New Nutshells

# Company Law
# in a Nutshell

*Other Titles in the Series*

**AUSTRALIA**
The Law Book Company Ltd.
Sydney : Melbourne : Brisbane

**CANADA AND U.S.A.**
The Carswell Company Ltd.
Agincourt, Ontario

**INDIA**
N.M. Tripathi Private Ltd.
Bombay
*and*
Eastern Law House Private Ltd.
Calcutta
M.P.P. House
Bangalore

**ISRAEL**
Steimatzky's Agency Ltd.
Jerusalem : Tel Aviv : Haifa

**MALAYSIA : SINGAPORE : BRUNEI**
Malayan Law Journal (Pte.) Ltd.
Singapore

**NEW ZEALAND**
Sweet and Maxwell (N.Z.) Ltd.
Auckland

**PAKISTAN**
Pakistan Law House
Karachi

New Nutshells

# Company Law in a Nutshell

Francis Roundell

London
Sweet & Maxwell
1980

*Published in 1980 by*
*Sweet & Maxwell Ltd. of*
*11 New Fetter Lane, London.*
*Set by CET Graphics of Cheltenham, Glos.*
*Printed in Great Britain by*
*J. W. Arrowsmith Ltd.,*
*London and Bristol*

**British Library Cataloguing in Publication Data**

Roundell, Francis
   Company law—(New nutshells).
   1. Corporation law—Great Britain
   I. Title II. Series
   346′.41′066   KD2057

   ISBN 0-421-26530-2

# Series Introduction

*New Nutshells* present the essential facts of law. Written in clear, uncomplicated language, they explain basic principles and highlight key cases and statutes.

*New Nutshells* meet a dual need for students of law or related disciplines. They provide a concise introduction to the central issues surrounding a subject, preparing the reader for detailed complementary textbooks. Then, they act as indispensable revision aids.

Produced in a convenient pocketbook format, *New Nutshells* serve both as invaluable guides to the most important questions of law and as reassuring props for the anxious examination candidate.

*Company Law* opens with an introduction to basic terminology before looking at promotion of companies, flotations, raising of capital, and shares. Separate chapters are devoted to insider dealing, corporate personality, and objects and powers of a company. Other topics explained include rights of members, management, liability for officers/agents and duties of directors. Concluding sections cover meetings, publicity, liquidations, and arrangements and reconstructions.

### Author's note

This book went to press in the expectation that the Companies Bill 1979 would become law as the Companies Act 1980. Section numbers in this book are taken from the clauses of the original bill. The new Act is also expected to contain further reforms, particularly relating to Insider Dealing.

To Lynda

# Contents

# 1 Introduction

Companies are usually formed by *registration* under the Companies Acts. The principal Act is the 1948 Act, a culmination of previous legislation and the Report of the Cohen Committee (1945). Except where the context indicates otherwise, section references in this book are to that Act. Subsequent Companies Acts were passed in 1967, 1976 and 1980, following proposals by the Jenkins Committee (1962) and, increasingly, the EEC, in its efforts to harmonise the company laws of its Member States.

Members of an *unlimited company* acquire the advantage of incorporation but their personal liability to creditors of the company is unlimited. Therefore, most companies are *limited companies*, with the liability of the members limited to the nominal value of the *shares* they hold or, less commonly, the amount they *guarantee* to contribute to the company's liability on liquidation. A registered company is a *public limited company* (which words must follow its name) if it is limited by shares or guarantee (or possibly both), its memorandum of association states it is a public company and it is so registered. Remaining registered companies are *private* companies. A private limited company must not offer its securities (shares or debentures) to the public. It may re-register as a public company by passing a special resolution and, *inter alia*, if its nominal share capital is not below the *authorised minimum* (currently £50,000) and at least one quarter of the nominal value of each share allotted has been

1

received. An unlimited company may re-register as a public company (and *vice versa*) and a public company may re-register as a private company. A member may incur unlimited liability if his company's membership falls below two.

*Registration*

For the registration of a company, delivery of certain documents to the Registrar of Companies is required. These include the *memorandum of association*, stating its name, situation of registered office, objects, whether it is limited or not and its initial share structure, and the *articles of association*, the terms regulating the association of the members, which will be on the terms of Table A in Schedule 1 to the 1948 Act unless otherwise excluded or modified. The memorandum of a public company must, as near as possible, follow the form in Schedule 1, Part I to the 1980 Act and its stated share capital must not be less than the authorised minimum. A statement of compliance with the statutory requirements and a statement of the company's first directors and secretary must accompany the application.

The Registrar must satisfy himself the statutory require-ments have been fulfilled and then register the company and issue a certificate of incorporation, stating it is incorporated and (if so) that it is a limited and a public company; the certificate is conclusive evidence of compliance with the statutory requirements and of the statements it contains. A public company initially registered as such cannot commence business until section 4 of the 1980 Act is complied with and the Registrar issues a *trading certificate*. The EEC proposes to enable companies in two or more Member States, satisfying criteria to be laid down, to combine as a *European Company* and to be effective as a company in each Member State.

# 2 Promotion of companies

A promoter is "one who undertakes to form a company
with reference to a given project and to set it going, and
who takes the necessary steps to accomplish that purpose."
He may be anyone who participates or has an interest in
setting up the company, bar someone involved in a purely
professional capacity, such as a solicitor. The promoters are
often the company's first directors.

*Liability of promoters*

A promoter may become liable to third parties for
misrepresentation or perhaps as the partner of another
promoter, under agency principles in partnership law.
Possibly, he will be liable to the new company under
contract or conceivably for deceit or negligence. The
traditional area of liability to the company is for breach of
the fiduciary duties he owes it during its promotion.

Equity will not permit him to take advantage of his
privileged position in relation to the unborn company. He
must make full disclosure to it, when formed, of his
interest in any transaction and must not profit from his
position without the company's free consent. Otherwise, he
must account personally for profits made and hold on
constructive trust any property received which came to him
by virtue of his being a promoter.

The rule is strict because, whatever the entitlement to

reward of a person whose enterprise results in the establishment of a company and the desirability of stimulating such enterprise, the promoter has an especial opportunity to divert to himself the benefits afforded to the company to be formed and to take advantage of potential investors.

Thus, a promoter who owns property before the promotion begins which he later sells to the company at a profit may retain the proceeds if he discloses all the facts. But, once promotion has begun, any property he acquires while in his fiduciary position will be held on trust for the company (subject to reimbursing him for the price) unless he clearly proves that he obtained the property solely in his personal capacity, for resale to the company on disclosing the full facts, although such proof might well fail if he should have obtained the property for the company directly.

He must disclose fully the nature and extent of his interest and profit. The duty cannot be avoided by setting up a company with a board of directors which cannot and does not "exercise an independent and intelligent judgment on the transaction" and disclosing merely to that board (*Erlanger* v. *New Sombrero*, 1878). The directors should not contribute to disadvantaging the shareholders. Disclosure to the members would be effective if they acquiesced (*Lagunas Nitrate* v. *Lagunas Syndicate*, 1899) but not if an undue advantage over potential investors remained, *e.g.* if the original members comprised or were otherwise under the influence of the promoters (*Gluckstein* v. *Barnes*, 1900).

*Remedies*

The company may be able to *rescind* a contract entered into consequent upon non-disclosure or misrepresentation by a promoter unless one of the bars to rescission has become operative, i.e. affirmation; lapse of time; intervening third party rights; inability to make *restitutio*

4

*in integrum*; and the court's discretion to award damages in lieu of rescission (Misrepresentation Act 1967, s.2(2)).

Breach of fiduciary duty may result in liability to *account* and/or imposition of a *constructive trust*. But promoters should be able to retain expenses incurred in acquiring property in such cases.

A slender thread of authority suggests that *damages* (a common law remedy) may be awarded for breach of fiduciary (equitable) duties (*Re Leeds & Hanley Theatres*, 1902; *Jacobus Marler* v. *Marler*, 1913). In principle, this is misconceived but the cases might be supported on the ground that promoters must refrain from deceit or negligence, the remedy for which is damages.

## Remuneration and expenses

The promoter does his work and incurs expenses, by the very nature of his position, at a time before the company has become legally capable of acting. Hence, it cannot enter into a binding agreement with him to remunerate him (or even to indemnify him for expenses) nor can the company, when formed, validly ratify (i.e. retrospectively validate) such an agreement made when it did not exist (*Kelner* v. *Baxter*, 1866). It cannot even enter into a new contract with him after formation (except under seal), for the consideration he provides will be past.

The practical solution is for promoters to secure the insertion in the articles of a provision enabling the directors (amongst whom will often be numbered willing promoters) to pay promoters expenses plus reasonable remuneration, which provision will be valid if full disclosure is made.

## Pre-incorporation contracts

Similar difficulties arise with contracts purporting to be made between the company and third parties before incorporation. The company will not normally be bound by preliminary contracts. Nor will the promoter be liable for breach of implied warranty of authority (for acting as the agent of a then non-existent principal) if no implication can be made, the third party knowing the true facts. The company may be liable apart from contract, to pay a reasonable amount for benefits actually received, or for conversion, for refusing to permit the third party to retake goods delivered.

Rather than attempting to bind the company, a promoter might contract personally with a third party and forward benefits received to the company when formed, under a separate contract. He might make the company liable on his original contract by assignment. In practice he often stipulates for his liability to cease if the company enters into an identical contract after incorporation: this is possible because if, as usual, the third party has outstanding obligations, he will not be providing merely past consideration (*Natal Land Co.* v. *Pauline Colliery*, 1904).

The precise role played by a promoter in entering preliminary contracts has proved decisive. Evidence of intention to secure a legally binding contract may shew a promoter's intention to contract personally even if he adds to his signature that he acts "on behalf of" the company to be formed (*Kelner* v. *Baxter*). But neither company nor promoter would be liable if the signature on the contract is supposedly that of the company itself alone (*Newborne* v. *Sensolid*, 1953). Is the wording of the recently enacted section 9(2) of the European Communities Act 1972 (hereafter, E.C.A.) necessarily sufficient to assist third parties?

"Where a contract purports to be made by a company, or by a person as agent for a company, at a time when the company has not been formed, then subject to any agreement to the contrary the contract shall have effect as a contract entered into by the person purporting to act for the company or as agent for it, and he shall be personally liable on the contract accordingly."

# 3 Flotations

A company may issue shares by various methods. It could invite tenders or subscriptions directly from the public (usually through the agency of an *issuing house*, of known standing). It might sell them to the issuing house, for it to resell them to the public, by issuing a prospectus or inviting subscriptions, or it might *place* them with the issuing house, either for sale and resale to selected clients of the issuing house or for inviting clients to subscribe. The issuing house is rewarded, where it buys shares, by its profit on resale, and otherwise by commission, especially where it underwrites an issue, by taking up itself any shares not otherwise disposed of. Any commission for underwriting an issue must not exceed 10 per cent., must be authorised by the articles and must be disclosed in the prospectus.

The Stock Exchange imposes rigorous requirements for securities to be listed. Parliament has generally contented itself with requirements for disclosure. The Prevention of Fraud (Investments) Act 1958, section 14 generally prohibits the distribution of a document containing an offer to dispose of or acquire securities without the consent of the Department of Trade except in certain cases (which cover most practical situations).

## Prospectuses

A prospectus is any document offering securities to the public for subscription or purchase, which includes offers for sale or placings. An offer calculated to result in shares becoming available other than to those receiving the offer or invitation is made to the public.

An application form for securities issued to the public must generally be issued only with a prospectus and any prospectus issued must set out auditors' and accountants' reports and state details of the number and price of shares, class rights, company property, material contracts, directors and their interests, promoters, commissions and expenses (s. 38). These details are unnecessary where shares are issued to existing members or are uniform with existing listed shares or where an application for listing is made and the Stock Exchange issues a certificate of exemption. If a prospectus contains an expert's report, his consent must be given and recorded. A copy of the prospectus must be delivered to the Registrar.

The prospectus requirements are inapplicable to the allotment or sale of shares for a non-cash consideration (*Government Stock* v. *Christopher*, 1956) or to subsequent dealings.

The practice of issuing shares using issuing house facilities and of obtaining Stock Exchange quotations for certain shares, with the corresponding necessity to comply in advance with the rules of the Issuing Houses Association and the Stock Exchange Requirements, restricts the potential liability of persons responsible for issuing shares, although the sanctions provide no legal redress. Criminal or civil liability may however arise.

*Criminal penalties*

The 1948 Act creates offences, punishable by fine and possibly imprisonment, for breach of certain of its provisions, *e.g.* issuing an application for securities without a prospectus (s. 38 (3)) or authorising the issue of a prospectus containing an untrue statement (s. 44). The Prevention of Fraud (Investments) Act 1958, s.13 makes it an offence to induce a person to invest money if the inducement is fraudulent or reckless (negligence is insufficient). It is similarly an offence fraudulently or recklessly (dishonestly or otherwise) to induce someone to deposit money with a company (Banking Act 1979, s. 39). Under the Theft Act 1968, s. 19, a company officer causing or contributing to publication of a statement knowing it to be false or misleading, with intent to deceive members or creditors, may be imprisoned. Those publishing false statements may also be convicted of common law conspiracy to defraud.

*Civil liability*

Whether on the first issue of or a subsequent dealing with shares, a person relying on a false statement may have a remedy against the company or the individual responsible (who may have to indemnify the company for liability arising from his misconduct).

A person subscribing for or purchasing shares on the basis of a misrepresentation may *rescind* the contract. Rescission is available against the company if it has knowledge that the contract is made on the basis of the representation, the misrepresentation is made in a prospectus deemed to be issued by the company and it is made within the authority of an agent of the company. The remedy is subject to the usual bars and to the court's discretion to award damages in lieu. Damages for breach of contract are unlikely to be available against the company, mainly because of the rules governing the maintenance of capital and equal rights of membership, but such damages might be claimed from a transferor of shares.

A person intended to rely and actually relying on a false representation made knowingly, or without belief in its truth, or recklessly (careless of whether it be true or false) may sue for damages for deceit (*Derry* v. *Peek*, 1889). But a purchaser of shares in the market cannot sue if the representation is made as an inducement only to original subscribers (*Peek* v. *Gurney*, 1873) unless it is also meant to mislead subsequent purchasers or is re-activated by a later statement (*Andrews* v. *Mockford*, 1896). It was held in *Houldsworth* v. *City of Glasgow Bank* (1880) that a shareholder cannot claim damages from the company while he remains a member (*i.e.* without terminating his membership or after rescission becomes impossible) as this would, apparently, result in a return of capital to a member (see Chap. 4). Is the decision sound?

A subscriber for shares on the faith of an untrue statement in a prospectus may claim compensation from persons authorising its issue, subject to defences of reasonable belief, ignorance or disclaimer (s. 43). He is, therefore, in a better position than a subsequent purchaser, who may be confined to damages for negligent misstatement under *Hedley Byrne* v. *Heller* (1964) or (so long as the defendant has contracted with him) under the Misrepresentation Act 1967, s. 2(1).

# 4 Raising and maintenance of capital

A company may finance its activities in a number of ways. It could simply obtain an overdraft from its bank or buy equipment on hire-purchase terms (or even lease it). For borrowing of substantial sums and/or for long-term borrowing, it will often issue *debentures* at a fixed rate of interest; their attraction will depend on their tax advantages and a comparison of levels of income derivable from interest and dividends on shares.

Shares provide the initial finance for most companies. Just as a company's securities may be divided into shares and debentures, so may there be ordinary shares and one or more classes of *preference share* to appeal to the desires of different investors. Different classes may be created on the company's formation, or at any later time (s. 61). Existing shareholders have pre-emption rights on the issue of new shares (1980 Act, s. 17).

The rights of any preference shareholder are limited to the terms of issue of his class of share. Thus, if he is entitled to a fixed rate of dividend, prima facie he cannot participate in remaining income; and if an annual dividend is not declared, only a *cumulative* preference shareholder can claim arrears. He may be paid off on a reduction of capital or, if his shares are redeemable, by redemption (in which case, a sum equal to their nominal value must be transferred to a *capital redemption reserve fund*) and he is not necessarily able to vote at meetings. In many respects his position is comparable to that of a debenture-holder.

## Capital

Share capital may be *nominal capital* (the amount of money its memorandum entitles a company to raise). This may comprise *issued share capital* (the shares actually issued) and unissued share capital. *Paid up capital* represents the money actually received from share issues and *uncalled capital* the amount still owed. *Reserve capital* is uncalled capital the company has resolved only to call up on liquidation. Most shares today are fully paid up and often worth more than their nominal value.

Shares may be issued at a premium (for more than their nominal value); if so the extra value is transferred to a *share premium account*. Profits undistributed as income are kept in a *reserve* fund. The nominal value of his shares, therefore, indicates the maximum the member has to contribute to the company's liabilities but says nothing about the company's worth (which is better indicated by their market price), especially as fixed assets lost need not be replaced. The company's share structure could, there-fore, be rationalised either by capitalising the sums in the share premium account and reserve fund and by issuing *bonus* shares to the existing shareholders, or by reducing capital (see Chap. 19).

## Raising capital

The liability of members of limited companies is limited to the nominal value of their shares. Certain rules help to ensure that this "creditors' guarantee fund" is not illusory. Thus, the nominal value of a public company's share capital must not be less than the authorised minimum, a quarter of which must be received before it can begin business (1980 Act, s. 4). One quarter of the nominal value of all issued shares of a public company plus any premiums must be paid up (1980 Act, s. 22). Shares must not be issued at a discount (s. 21), although debentures may (unless they are immediately convertible into equal value shares). A commission may be paid to underwriters. Shares may be allotted for money or money's worth but a public company's shares can only be allotted to original subscribers for cash and, if allotted for money's worth, the allottee must receive from the company an expert's valuation of the consideration (ss. 20-31).

*Maintenance of capital*

Prima facie, capital cannot be returned to members by the company (though, of course, they might recoup their investment by selling shares to others). Thus, a company cannot acquire its own shares, a practice which would enable directors to manipulate share values, depending on the price paid for shares the company bought. Nor must it provide financial assistance to another to acquire its or its holding company's shares (1948 Act, s. 54). A loan for that purpose and any guarantee of the loan (*Heald* v. *O'Connor*, 1971) will be void (*Selangor* v. *Cradock (No. 3)*, 1968); the company and its officers may be fined; and participating directors are liable to the company for misfeasance and breach of trust (*Wallersteiner* v. *Moir*, 1974).

The inevitable risk to capital in business is recognised, however. Losses to *fixed assets* (*e.g.* a mine) need not normally be made good before profits are distributed (*Lee* v. *Neuchatel*, 1889). Losses to *circulating assets* (*e.g.* stock-in-trade) for previous accounting periods may be written off. Dividends may only be distributed out of *profits* (*i.e.* out of unutilised realised profits less accumulated realised losses, so far as not previously written off: 1980 Act, s. 39) and provided the amount of the net assets do not become less than the aggregate of the company's called-up share capital and its undistributable reserves (s. 40). Unrealised profits may only be issued as bonus shares (s. 45(1)) but an

13

unrealised profit on the revaluation of a fixed asset may, after provision for depreciation, be included among the realised profits (s. 39(5)). An extraordinary general meeting must be called in the event of net assets falling to half of a company's called-up share capital (s. 34).

*Dividends*

Subject to the above and to current economic restraints (*e.g.* Dividends Act 1978), dividends may be declared as provided by the articles, which generally authorise the directors to make or recommend declarations. Members are prima facie entitled to participate equally in dividends and can sue for them once declared. Although distributions may not be made in the absence of profits, a preference share-holder whose shares entitle him to dividends regardless of declaration may prove for arrears on liquidation (*Re New Chinese Antimony*, 1916).

# 5 Shares

A person may become a shareholder by subscribing to the memorandum and having one or more shares allotted to him, or by having shares transferred to him by an existing shareholder, or by applying for shares and having them allotted to him (generally in response to a prospectus). An allottee has a contractual right to be registered which, under a renounceable letter of allotment, he can renounce (assign) in favour of a third party (who pays him for it).

Companies must keep a register of the class and extent of members' shareholdings which is open to inspection and is prima facie evidence of the details therein. A member may hold shares or a proportion of *stock* (into which paid-up shares may be converted). But a shareholder with a *share warrant* (a negotiable instrument, transferable by delivery and carrying a right to a certain number of shares) is not normally considered to be a member and is not entered as such on the register.

A share is an item of property and normally freely transferable. It gives its holder an interest in the company measured by a sum of money (representing the prima facie extent of his liability to creditors) and entitling him to the rights contained in the articles. The value of shares is generally their market price (*Short* v. *Treasury Commissioners*, 1948), although a large number whose votes confer control may be worth more.

## Preference shares

Prima facie, shareholders have equal rights but a company can alter its articles to issue another class of shares carrying preferential rights (*Andrews* v. *Gas Meter*, 1897), in which case a presumption of equality applies to those aspects where there is no preference (*e.g.* a right to a preferential dividend does not exclude the right to equal participation in capital on liquidation: *Birch* v. *Cropper*, 1889).

A preference which does exist is deemed to be exhaustive: so a member entitled to a preferential dividend may not participate in the remaining profits (*Will* v. *United Lankat*, 1913) and one entitled on liquidation to a return of capital subscribed may not participate in remaining assets (*Scottish Insurance* v. *Wilsons & Clyde*, 1949). Moreover, undistributed profits which are capitalised are treated on liquidation as capital and not as undistributed dividends (*Dimbula* v. *Laurie*, 1961). Where preference shareholders not entitled to participate in surplus assets on winding-up are paid off because of a reduction in capital, their only entitlement is to the nominal, not the market, value of their shares (*Re Chatterley-Whitfield*, 1949).

## Calls and liens

A share in a public company must be paid up by at least 25 per cent. (1980 Act, s. 22) but the company can make calls on the holder up to the unpaid value. The articles may give the company a lien over the share for calls on the holder up to the unpaid value. They often empower it to forfeit the share for unpaid calls; problems are rare since most shares are fully paid up.

A lien is an equitable charge on the share. It becomes effective on a specified event (*e.g.* for calls—immediately shares are issued). Thus, a different equitable interest of which the company has notice overrides a lien for debts due from the member (which it could set-off against dividends) if the member only becomes indebted after that interest arose. Once a lien does become effective, it binds a third party acquiring a later equitable interest, as he has constructive notice of the articles giving the lien.

## Share certificates

A company must within two months of the allotment of shares or debentures or within two months of the lodging of a transfer of such securities, complete certificates, unless otherwise provided in their original issue (s. 80) or unless the allotment is to, or the lodging of transfer is with, a Stock Exchange nominee (Stock Exchange (Completion of Bargains) Act 1976, s. 1). A share certificate is prima facie evidence that the person therein named was at the time of issue a shareholder and registered as such (1948 Act, s. 81) and the company is estopped from denying its statement as against a person relying on it (who might be able to recover damages if the statement were untrue: *Re Bahia Railway*, 1868). Thus, a company cannot make calls on shares it certifies as fully paid up. The estoppel may be available to the person to whom the certificate is issued as well as to subsequent parties (*Balkis* v. *Tomkinson*, 1893). But it will not avail a person who has not relied on the representation or who has put forward a forged transfer to the company.

## Transfer and transmission of securities

Shares are normally freely transferable. But the articles may restrict transfer, in which case a refusal to register must be made within two months of its being lodged (s. 78) and must not be made in bad faith (*Re Smith & Fawcett*, 1942). Normally, shares are transferred by sale, in which case the transferor's liability to the transferee depends on contractual principles.

The seller should transfer his share certificate to the buyer so that the company will readily consent to registering him as a member. If the seller only transfers part of his holding he should deposit his share certificate with the

Stock Exchange (for quoted shares) or the company, which will issue a certificate of transfer, stating that a share certificate covering the relevant shares has been deposited (*George Whitechurch* v. *Cavanagh*, 1902). It does not necessarily represent that there has been a transfer or that the transferee is entitled to the shares (*Bishop* v. *Balkis*, 1890). It operates as a representation by the company to a person acting on it that documents have been produced to it showing the transferor's prima facie title to the securities specified (s. 79).

For a transfer to be registered, an instrument of transfer must be delivered to the company (s. 75), by either the transferor or transferee. The transferor does not guarantee registration, in the absence of which he holds the shares on trust for the transferee. A person presenting a forged transfer must indemnify the company for loss it suffers (*Welch* v. *Bank of England*, 1955). If the register is altered in consequence, the true shareholder may be reinstated and compensated for loss suffered. The company may be liable for statements therein in a resulting share certificate.

An unregistered transferee, having only an equitable interest, takes subject to other equitable interests of which he has notice when he acquires his interest. But if equitable interests are equal, the first to register, and to acquire the legal interest, prevails. Otherwise, the first in time has priority, unless a subsequent claimant acquires a right against the company to be registered before it receives notice of a further claim (*Peat* v. *Clayton*, 1906).

# 6 Insider dealing

Controversy has been generated over the use of confidential information affecting the value of securities which is taken into account by the person in possession of it in deciding whether to buy or sell shares, so as to make a future profit or avoid an impending loss. The ability to do this has been defended as the entrepreneur's just reward and as helping the price of securities to reflect their true worth. More often, "insider trading" is seen to be commercially immoral as giving the insider an unfair advantage over other investors. How could it be prevented?

One possibility is to require *disclosure* of such information. But the insider may be under a confidential duty not to disclose. If he had to disclose, should he do so only to the person with whom he is dealing or to the public in general? And is merely requiring disclosure sufficient for the other party without an additional remedy?

A further possibility is to enable the "outsider" to *rescind* the contract. Another is to try to eliminate the profit motive by making an insider *account* for his unfair profit. But to whom? If to the company, the company may resolve not to call him to account. If it did and he were a member, he would derive some benefit anyway. But the company may have suffered no loss and accounting to the company would not compensate the outsider, who would be difficult to identify if it were an anonymous Stock Exchange transaction. Moreover, whatever remedy an outsider were to seek, he might find it difficult to prove to

19

what extent, if any, the use of the inside information affected the transaction. And should an outsider who dealt with an insider be in a better position than one who dealt with another person not in possession of such information?

Some have argued that the only real deterrent is to impose criminal liability for insider dealing, a method which could unfortunately ban legitimate dealings where there was no abuse of the inside information, by persons who are after all dealing with their own securities. It could also discourage persons who at present freely co-operate in Department of Trade investigations but who would not wish to run the risk of implication—so how could the criminal penalties be enforced?

Is then a better solution self-restraint and self-regulation? The Stock Exchange rules, the Model Code for Securities Transactions, the disciplinary powers of the Exchange and under the Take-Over Panel may go a long way to alleviating the problem. But they do not give an individual *locus standi* to enforce the rules, nor do they help an outsider not dealing in the market. Similarly, administrative control by the Department of Trade is arguably of little use to individuals and may be thought ineffective without adequate supportive criminal sanctions.

The current position in England reflects a combination of these solutions.

The common law position is based on *Percival* v. *Wright* (1902). Shareholders offered to sell shares to directors who knew their true value was greater because of an impending take-over bid, which information their confidential obligations to the company forbade them to disclose. For that reason it was decided that the shareholders could not rescind the contract. The directors had no general duty to the shareholders to disclose price-sensitive information to them. The United States courts have generally circum-vented the decision by extending the categories of "special circumstances" requiring disclosure. Not so for the English courts, although it was held in *Allen* v. *Hyatt* (1914) that directors exercising options to buy members' shares granted prior to a merger should account to those members for profits made, since in negotiating the sale of the shares to the take-over bidder they were acting as the members' agents. In New Zealand, in *Coleman* v. *Myers* (1977), a director was liable to shareholders in a small family company where a fiduciary duty to them arose because of the special relationship.

The Companies Act 1967 does three things. It imposes a statutory prohibition by making it a criminal offence for a director to purchase an option to buy or sell quoted shares or debentures of a company in his group (s. 25). This liability is extended to his wife and children unless they had no reason to believe he was a director (s. 30).

Secondly, it enacts requirements for disclosure and publicity. A director must (subject to a fine and/or imprisonment) disclose to the company details concerning the acquisition or disposal of any beneficial interest of himself, his wife or children in the securities of the group (ss. 25, 31), such information having to be made available (s. 29). If the shares are quoted, the company must pass the information on to the Stock Exchange, which may publish it (1976 Act, s. 25). Any shareholder with a prescribed percentage of shares (currently 5 per cent.) in a quoted company must notify it of the acquisition and disposal of shares in the company carrying unrestricted voting rights, which information is again made available (1967 Act, ss. 33-34).

Thirdly, there is some administrative control. Under section 32 of the 1967 Act, the Department of Trade can appoint inspectors to investigate suspected breaches of sections 25, 27 and 31. Leave to prosecute under sections 27 and 33, and section 25 of the 1976 Act, must be given by the Secretary of State, who may also exempt persons from having to comply with section 27 of the 1976 Act (enabling companies to require disclosure of beneficial interests in their voting shares).

It has been suggested that the Prevention of Fraud (Investments) Act 1958, s. 13 imposes a duty, enforceable through the criminal law, to make a full disclosure of information relevant to a particular securities transaction where a failure to do so would be considered dishonest, the dishonesty being found in the intentional exploitation of the privileged information to the injury of the other party. This provision could be important in private dealings (there is less likely to be an "inducement" in market dealings) but only provides for criminal liability.

# 7 Debentures

A company may borrow money by means of debentures, documents evidencing the amount of the debt. Instead of a series of debentures for a number of separate debts, it may create one fund of debenture stock and issue certificates for particular divisions of the fund. In many ways, a debenture-holder is as much an investor as a shareholder. But a shareholder is a member of the company whereas a debenture-holder is a creditor, whatever the similarities or dissimilarities between the rights and obligations of the two. The law governing the transfer of the securities held by shareholders and debenture-holders is basically similar, apart from the fact that debentures must be transferred as a whole (therefore there is no need to certify transfers of them) and are generally transferable without limitation (bearer debentures are negotiable instruments). In other respects, the law differs.

*Rights of debenture-holders*
Whereas the articles of association can be varied, the rights of debenture-holders are fixed by the contract of loan and any attempted variation of them by the company (other than under a compromise or arrangement) will be a breach of contract. Hence, although the articles of association are alterable by statute so that an alteration cannot be restrained by injunction, a declaration may be granted that an alteration of articles on which the debenture contract is based is nevertheless a breach of that contract (*Baily v.*

*British Equitable*, 1904). And the court might exercise its discretion to grant to a debenture-holder an injuction to restrain the company from acting according to the articles as altered ( *e.g.* if such action would weaken his position by putting the company's capital at risk). If the breach of contract were sufficiently serious, the debenture-holder might be justified in terminating his contract with the company and claiming repayment of his investment plus interest. In these cases, a debenture-holder can bring a debenture-holder's action on behalf of the debenture holders. But these remedies are only necessary for holders of unsecured ("naked") debentures. More often, debentures will be issued so as to give their holders the improved remedies provided by some form of security.

## Charges

One possibility is for the company to create a *fixed charge* over certain of its property for the amount of the loan. This is reasonably simple in respect of certain forms of property (*e.g.* a mortgage of buildings). But it is inappropriate for fluctuating assets (*e.g.* raw materials and finished products), which may constitute a large part of the company's assets (and so a major means of providing security) but which the company must be able to transfer freely and with unencumbered title if it is to carry on business efficiently. The difficulty has been overcome by the invention of the *floating charge*.

A floating charge floats over the whole or a part of the company's assets, which may fluctuate as disposals and acquisitions are made free of the charge. The theory is either that the lender has a current charge and licences the company to deal with the property freely until crystallisation or that it is a charge of the assets actually in the hands of the company at the time of crystallisation. The charge *crystallises* on the occurrence of a specified event (automatically on a winding-up), in which case it becomes a fixed charge over assets then in the company's possession.

Its value as security then depends, of course, on the assets remaining in the company's possession, so it is not uncommonly provided that a receiver may be appointed in certain circumstances to safeguard the interests of debenture-holders if they are at risk. This is usually done by trustees for debenture-holders, in whom legal title to debentures is commonly vested so that there is one small body which can exercise rights on behalf of a variety of debenture-holders.

A charge must be *registered* within 21 days of its creation or the acquisition of property subject to it. Registration may be effected by any interested person. On receipt of the required details, the Registrar must enter them on the register and issue a certificate, which is conclusive evidence of compliance with the statutory requirements. The company and any officer at fault may be fined for non-registration. The court has a discretion to extend the registration period (s. 101) but a first chargee who registers late will not get priority over a registered second charge unless it was created within 21 days of the first (*Watson v. Duff*, 1974).

Section 95 lists the registrable charges, including those for securing issues of debentures, on land, on the company's book debts and floating charges. Not every charge is registrable: an unpaid vendor's lien is not, being a creation of law and not arising from contract. Where a supplier delivers goods to the company on the basis that legal and equitable ownership remain in the supplier and that the goods (whether in the same or modified form) may be sold by the company as the supplier's agent, the restriction is not registrable as the goods do not become the property of the company and the restriction is not created by it (*Aluminium v. Romalpa*, 1976; *Borden v. Scottish Timber*, 1979). By this means, suppliers can secure themselves and deprive the company of assets which may become subject to an existing floating charge. Where the supplier retains only the beneficial title, this amounts to the creation of a registrable equitable floating charge (*Re Bond Worth*, 1979).

Where a registrable charge created by the company is not registered, the security is void against other creditors (s. 95). Thus, a later chargee may register his charge and gain priority over an unregistered earlier charge of which he is aware. The unregistered chargee may still enforce his security against the company; moreover, on failure to register, the company becomes liable to repay him his loan immediately. A charge over land which is registered according to section 95 should also be registered with the Land Registry or Land Charges Registry to be fully effective.

If registered in compliance with the statutory requirements, the charge is valid according to the terms of its creation, even though all the details do not have to be registered. Registration constitutes constructive notice of the existence of a charge but not necessarily of its contents. Thus a subsequent chargee is unaffected by an unregistered restriction on the creation of subsequent charges (*Wilson* v. *Kelland*, 1910).

*Priorities of charges*

A registered charge in general gives the chargee a prior right, according to its terms, over a subsequent charge and any previous unregistered charge. But a subsequent floating charge can be created over a particular part of the assets covered by a previous floating charge over the wider category (*Re Automatic Bottle Makers*, 1926). And a later fixed charge will gain priority over a previous floating charge covering the assets in question. In either case, this is because floating charges are created with knowledge of the possibility of subsequent dealings with assets.

On crystallisation, a floating chargee can only enforce his security over property which is not otherwise subject to existing rights. Thus, a debtor of the company can maintain a right of set-off which he has at the time of crystallisation

(*Biggerstaff* v. *Rowatt's Wharf*, 1896) but not one he acquires after the chargees' rights have crystallised (*Robbie* v. *Witney*, 1963).

An existing registered charge, even if it prohibits the creation of subsequent charges, will not have priority over a charge already existing over after-acquired property, or created in order to acquire it (*e.g.* to secure payment of purchase moneys), for the property might not otherwise have been acquired (*Security Trust* v. *Royal Bank of Canada*, 1976).

Unregistered chargees may prove in a company's liquidation as unsecured creditors and rank in priority as such. Fixed chargees can simply enforce their security according to the terms of the charge. The rights of floating chargees are, however, postponed to those entitled to preferential payments on a winding-up (s. 94). A floating charge created within 12 months of liquidation is, unless the company was solvent immediately after its creation, void except to the amount of any cash paid simultaneously with or subsequently to its creation, plus interest. (s. 322) and may be attacked as a fraudulent preference if redeemed within six months of liquidation (*Re Parke's Garage*, 1929).

*Receivers*

Debentures often expressly provide that a receiver may be appointed on the occurrence of a specified event rendering the security enforceable. Receivers may also be appointed under an implied power or the court's inherent power. A receiver must generally get in the assets charged and collect any income due on them. He may realise the assets and pay the proceeds in reduction of the amount owed to the debenture-holders. He may also petition for liquidation. Usually it will be better for the company to continue trading and to appoint a receiver as *manager* of the company as well.

The mere appointment of a receiver and manager out of

court does not automatically terminate the employment of the directors or even prevent them from continuing to act, so long as that is not inconsistent with the powers of the receiver and the interests of the debenture-holders (*Newhart* v. *Co-operative Bank*, 1978). The commencement of winding-up may deprive the receiver of power to bind the company but he may continue to deal with the property securing the debenture (*Sowman* v. *Samuel*, 1978).

A receiver appointed by the court is an officer of the court and a receiver appointed by debenture-holders is in principle their agent. It is common to provide that a receiver and manager shall be the agent of the company, in which case he can exercise such powers as the directors can normally exercise. Thus, if the directors are not empowered to petition for winding-up, neither is the receiver exercising their powers, unless he is able to do so on another ground (*Re Emmadart*, 1979).

A receiver is not bound by the company's existing contracts. However, he and the company are liable on contracts made by him, although he may claim an indemnity from the company.

# 8 Corporate personality

A registered limited liability company is recognised in law as a person, with capacity to act as such, although of course not necessarily in the same way that a human being can act. Moreover, the company's personality is distinct from that of each and all of its members, albeit there may be similarities.

The leading case is *Salomon* v. *Salomon* (1897). Salomon formed a company with 20,007 shares. Each of six members of his family held one share as his nominees; he held the rest. He sold his existing business to the company in return for the shares and debentures issued to him for £10,000, thereby making him a secured creditor for that sum. The company quickly went into liquidation and its unsecured creditors, whose claims could not be met in full, tried to press their claims against Salomon himself on the basis that the company was his *alter ego* or agent. Those claims failed. The requirements of the legislation for setting up the company had been complied with and it was immaterial that Salomon held all the shares beneficially. The company had been established as a separate entity and it was that, not Salomon, with which the creditors had contracted.

By incorporation, therefore, a veil may be said to be drawn between persons dealing with a company and its members, so that direct proceedings may not generally be taken against the members themselves. Just as a third party cannot proceed against the members by ignoring the company, he may be similarly unable to proceed against the company through the medium of one of its members. In *B v. B* (1978), a wife was unable to obtain discovery of company documents by asking the court to order her husband, who had a right as a director to inspect them, to produce them.

The corporate personality rule may operate to the disadvantage of the members. A member cannot insure the company's property against destruction—it is not his property (*Macaura v. Northern Assurance*, 1925); but he may have an insurable interest in the venture in which the company is engaged.

If, therefore, individuals decide to become members of a limited liability company they must accept the adverse as well as the beneficial consequences of incorporation. They benefit from being able to trade with their liability limited to the value of their shares and they may be able to obtain tax advantages from investing in this form of business association. For members who merely wish to invest in, rather than to participate in the running of, a business enterprise, it is convenient to put their money into a company, the day-to-day activities of which can be carried on by an appointed board of directors. As an independent entity, the company can conduct litigation on its own behalf, as plaintiff or defendant, and may buy, hold or sell property without reference to the individual members. In particular, it can do these things perpetually for, unlike its members, it does not have to die (although it may be wound up). By offering these advantages, the law induces investment and encourages trade.

But at a price. The shareholder, depending on the size of his shareholding, is generally able to participate to some extent in company decisions by voting at meetings but he must bow to the will of the majority if that goes against him. His rights depend in part on articles of association which may be altered. His rights may be varied or he may even be paid off. Yet he cannot himself decide to leave the company and to recover the capital he invested, except insofar as he is free to sell his shares to another, who takes his place. If a minority shareholder, he receives protection in a number of forms, *e.g.* as a consequence of the publicity requirements in the companies legislation, but that may also be seen as an intrusion into otherwise private affairs. Similarly, the rights of members may be protected in liquidations, but the whole procedure of winding-up is an arduous and expensive way of terminating the company.

*Lifting the veil*

Although *Salomon* is still good law, there are a large number of cases in which the veil of corporate personality may be said to be lifted, so as to expose the identity of the company's members or officers. On one hand, it may be said that the number of exceptions has become so numerous that *Salomon* has been reduced to a shadow. On the other, it may be possible to find some consistency between those "exceptions" and *Salomon*.

The companies legislation contains numerous examples where *Salomon* is ignored. If the members fall below the statutory minimum, the remaining members may be personally liable for the company's debts (s. 31) and persons guilty of fraudulent trading may incur unlimited personal liability for the company's debts (s. 332). These cases may be seen as exceptions to *Salomon* or as cases where the parties have not fulfilled conditions upon which the privilege of limited liability is granted.

The courts may be faced with an unintended apparent conflict between *Salomon*, as a consequence of the Companies Acts, and the provisions of another Act of Parliament. Thus, compulsory purchase legislation normally entitles a person whose property is acquired or who is dispossessed to compensation. In *D.H.N.* v. *Tower Hamlets*

(1976) D.H.N. carried on a business on land owned by a subsidiary company, Bronze. The land was compulsorily acquired and compensation paid to Bronze. Compensation for disturbance was also payable to someone with an interest in the land. But no business of Bronze was disturbed and D.H.N. appeared to have no interest in the land. The Court of Appeal held D.H.N. to be entitled to compensation on the basis of the common factors in the identity of the group of companies. Otherwise, because of the companies' separate legal personalities, compensation would not have been payable in a case in which it clearly should have been. A similar result was reached in *Smith, Stone & Knight* v. *Birmingham* (1939) by declaring a subsidiary carrying on business on property of a holding company to be the latter's agent, thereby entitling it to compensation. *D.H.N.* was, however, disapproved in the distinguishable Scottish case of *Woolfson* v. *Strathclyde* (1978) H.L.

It may be that a strict application of *Salomon* may result in giving effect to Parliament's intention in another statute. In *Lee* v. *Lee's Air Farming* (1961), a widow received compensation for the death of her husband as an *employee* of the company, albeit he was sole governing director and held 2,999 of the 3,000 shares, because it followed from *Salomon* that he could function as an officer of his company and as an employee.

Apart from unintentionally enacting a statutory provision inconsistent with *Salomon*, there is, of course, no reason why the legislature cannot exercise its sovereign power directly to override *Salomon*. Thus, it can impose on the shareholders of a "close" company liability for advance corporation tax which is avoided by not distributing "relevant income" as dividend (Finance Act 1972).

A statute may give the courts discretion as to whether the corporate veil may be pierced. Hence, where an application is made to wind up a company on the "just and equitable" ground, the court may subject the exercise of

32

the members' legal rights to equitable considerations (see Chap. 18).

The courts have not infrequently taken it upon themselves to lift the veil. Their aim is usually seen to be the avoidance of clear injustice, although it is not obvious where the line may be drawn between apparent injustice which permits lifting of the veil and that which does not. (Is it arguable in any (or all) of the following situations that they are cases to which *Salomon* should not apply anyway?)

Corporate decisions are generally ineffective if the correct procedure is not followed. But if the only result of insisting on the correct procedure being pursued is counter-productive, it may be waived. In *Re Bailey Hay* (1971), a resolution by a minority (two) of the corporators was valid although the meeting was held at too short notice, because all five corporators attended and those not voting acquiesced in the resolution.

Certainly, considerations of public policy are likely to override particular legal rules. The courts are particularly unwilling to permit the use of the corporate form in order to further improper conduct. They may go farther. In *Gilford* v. *Horne* (1933), not only did the court grant an injunction against a former employee who had covenanted with his employers not to solicit their customers after he left their employment; it also granted an injunction against the company he set up (albeit he was not a member) in order to carry on a business inconsistent with the covenant. Similarly, a director cannot avoid the statutory provision prohibiting loans to directors by getting the company to lend money to a puppet company of his (*Wallersteiner* v. *Moir*, 1974).

The same approach may be used to avoid liability in "quasi-criminal" cases. A club which was an incorporated company was treated as an unincorporated association of individuals in *Trebanog* v. *Macdonald* (1904) so that its sales of liquor were matters of internal accounting, between the members, whose property the liquor was deemed to be, rather than a criminal retail sale without a licence.

The courts have also avoided the effects of *Salomon* by use of the concepts of trust and agency. In *The Abbey, Malvern Wells* v. *M.L.G.P.* (1951), the company's property was impressed with the terms of a trust where the shareholders and directors were trustees under a trust deed; in effect, the company was an incorporated charitable trust.

*Salomon* decided that a company is not generally the agent of its members. But the courts may be willing to admit an agency relationship between companies in the same group. In *Smith, Stone & Knight* v. *Birmingham* (1939), Alkinson J. enumerated the following tests, in deciding that a subsidiary company was the agent of its holding company: (i) whether the profits were treated as profits of the parent company; (ii) whether the persons conducting the business were appointed by the parent company; (iii) whether the parent company was the head and brain of the business; (iv) whether the parent company governed the adventure; (v) whether profits were made by the parent company's skill and direction; and (vi) whether the parent company was in effectual and constant control.

*Groups*

Just as individual human beings may combine for purposes of trade, so may different companies. But does it necessarily follow that because the law prima facie recognises an incorporated company as an independent legal person that it must concede completely independant character to each member of a group of companies? The reality of group structure, whether it arises historically or by decision (*e.g.* for convenience or tax advantages), finds expression in the definition of a subsidiary of a holding company as *either* a company in which the holding company is a member which either controls the composition of its board of directors or holds more than half in nominal value of its equity share capital *or* a subsidiary of another subsidiary of the holding company (s. 154).

From this definition it can be ascertained, *e.g.* whether group accounts, as well as separate accounts of each company, must be prepared, so as to provide a true and fair view of the state of affairs and profit or loss of the group as a whole. In *Wallersteiner* v. *Moir* (1974), a complicated arrangement of companies, trusts and so on, controlled by one man for his own purposes, was treated as a whole to see whether financial provision had been provided by a company for purchase of its own shares in contravention of section 54 (Chap. 4).

In *Holdsworth* v. *Caddies* (1955), the managing director of a holding company could not claim damages for breach of contract when ordered to confine his activities to the business of a subsidiary. In *Levison* v. *Farin* (1978), damages payable to a subsidiary were reduced by the amount of a tax benefit which shareholders would derive from a holding company, otherwise they would have benefited twice.

*Character of the corporate person*

Despite the separation of the company from its members, it may be necessary to look at the members to ascertain some details about the company itself. In *Daimler* v. *Continental Tyre* (1916) a company incorporated in England with a British subject (who had one share) as its Secretary could not sue in the English courts in wartime because the controllers (all the directors and the other shareholders) were enemy aliens, resident in Germany. Thus, residence, domicile or nationality may be gleaned from the identity of the members.

Companies are formed to carry on business. They may act through servants or agents but the acts of one of a company's organs (see Chapter 12) may be identified with acts of the company itself. Thus, the acts of a managing director, as the company's "directing mind and will," may be attributed to the company: *Lennard's Carrying* v. *Asiatic Petroleum* (1915). Hence, the corporate person is able to form an intention (*Bolton* v. *Graham*, 1956).

It does not necessarily follow that because a company is capable of action and has legal personality that it must be equated with natural persons (not all of whom have the same legal capacity anyway). Thus, whereas a company may enter into a partnership with an entertainer to do things which only a natural person can do (*Newstead* v. *Frost*, 1978), it cannot worship so as to enable it to breach the Sunday Observance Act 1677 (*Rolloswin* v. *Chromolit*, 1970).

# 9 Objects and powers

A company's memorandum of association not only indicates the objects which it is intended the company should pursue and the powers expressly conferred upon it to enable it to achieve those objects. It is also taken to state the prima facie extent of its powers, so that anything else done by the company is *ultra vires*, outside its powers, and something it is legally incapable of doing. So much is this the case that it cannot ratify in general meeting something which is done *ultra vires* (*Ashbury Railway* v. *Riche*, 1875). It should first alter its memorandum to give itself the necessary powers, if that is possible.

The reasons for the *ultra vires* doctrine are basically twofold. Shareholders who invest money in a company are entitled to see that it is applied for the purposes for which they are presumably induced to invest and not to see it dissipated in uncontemplated ventures. And those who advance credit to a company are entitled to rely on its creditworthiness so far as that can be ascertained from, *inter alia*, its statement of objects and powers.

However, the strength of the doctrine has been eroded so much by the ingenuity of draftsmen of memoranda of association, with the compliance of the courts, the power to alter the memorandum and the enactment of E.C.A. s. 9(1) that the doctrine has become less of a protection for members and creditors and more of an obstacle that may arise unexpectedly to invalidate an apparently *intra vires* transaction.

*Extent of the company's powers*

The company will be authorised to pursue its actual objects if they are clearly stated in the memorandum. Thus, a company empowered "to carry on all kinds of financial commercial trading or other operations" and "to enter into partnership with any person carrying on any business which this company is authorised to carry on" could enter into a partnership with the entertainer David Frost to exploit his services "as a producer, actor, director, writer and artiste," albeit the company itself could not directly carry out those activities (*Newstead* v. *Frost*, 1978).

A company can also do anything which is incidental to its stated objects (*A.G.* v. *Great Eastern Railway*, 1880). Thus, a company empowered to run railways could hire out rolling stock to other railways.

A company's express powers can be extended by including a great number of stated objects, even if it is not intended to pursue them all. In such a case, the court might feel constrained to allow as objects only those which it can interpret as its main objects and to confine the other "objects" to the status of powers which enable it to carry out its main objects. But if the stated objects are all expressly declared to be independent of each other, the court will normally acknowledge each "object" to be as valid as another (*Cotman* v. *Brougham*, 1918).

It will not even generally challenge the motive for which a given power is exercised. Thus, a charge given to a creditor which is in reality to further the interest of the directors may be held valid (*Charterbridge* v. *Lloyds Bank*, 1970).

Despite the apparent willingness of the judges to extend the limits of the *ultra vires* doctrine, it does not follow that they will permit any attempt by the company to evade its restrictions. So, the object of carrying on business as "merchants generally" is valid (*Re New Finance*, 1975) but an independent power to do anything whatsoever that the company desired may well be confined to the position of an incidental power on the basis that the "object" would be no object at all. A judge faced with the issue might conceivably capitulate on the basis that it is the function of the Registrar to decide whether or not to register a memorandum with such an object clause.

A more specific object may possibly not be upheld as an independent object. In *Re Introductions* (1969), it was held that a clause enabling the company to borrow money or to give guarantees could only create a power, because the most apparent result of exercising the clause would be to the company's disadvantage rather than advantage.

An incidental power may be similarly restricted. Hence, a gratuitous payment to employees may be made if it is to the obvious benefit of the company, such as to encourage productivity (*Hampson* v. *Price's Patent Candle*, 1876), but not if there is no clear advantage. A payment to employees who lost their jobs because the company ceased business was disallowed in *Parke* v. *Daily News*, 1962); power to make such payments is now implied (1980 Act, s. 46).

E.C.A. section 9(1) provides:

> "In favour of a person dealing with a company in good faith, any transaction decided on by the directors shall be deemed to be one which it is within the capacity of the company to enter into, and the powers of the directors to bind the company shall be deemed to be free of any limitation under the memorandum or articles of association; and a party to a transaction so decided on shall not be bound to enquire as to the capacity of the company to enter into it or as to any such limitation on the powers of the directors, and shall be presumed to have acted in good faith unless the contrary is proved."

The section arguably does away with the *ultra vires* doctrine for most practical purposes so far as persons dealing with the company are concerned. But the difficulties of its interpretation (*e.g.* when a transaction is "decided on by the directors") require clarification.

*Effect of the ultra vires rule*

If section 9(1) does not apply, a third party has to fall back on his rights at common law, under which the contract is prima facie unenforceable (*Re Jon Beauforte*, 1952), although, if the lender is unaware of the *ultra vires* purpose, repayment of a loan is enforceable to the extent that it could have been applied for *intra vires* purposes (*Re David Payne*, 1904). Otherwise, the third party may be able to trace money paid or property delivered to the company (*Sinclair* v. *Brougham*, 1914) or be subrogated to the rights of *intra vires* creditors paid off with the money; if he is a secured lender, he should be able to enforce his security (*Blackburn* v. *Cunliffe*, 1882).

A guarantee of an unenforceable loan can be enforced against the guarantor (*Heald* v. *O'Connor*, 1971). Moreover, a person who has fraudulently or negligently induced someone to enter into an *ultra vires* transaction with the company may be liable to the latter for deceit or negligence.

The company can be restrained by its members by injunction from entering into an *ultra vires* transaction. But once it has entered into one, it is not clear whether or not it can enforce it. It cannot do so under E.C.A., section 9(1) because that section only operates in favour of the other party. It has recently been suggested that the third party can plead *ultra vires* as a defence (*Bell Houses* v. *City Wall*, 1966).

*Alteration of the memorandum*

A company can confer validity on a transaction in advance by altering its memorandum of association by special resolution for all or any of the purposes specified in section 5, *e.g.* carrying on its business more economically or efficiently, acquiring new or improved powers, changing its area of operations, restricting or abandoning any of the objects in the memorandum or combining with another company. The list is wide enough for most purposes, but an alteration is not covered for a purpose not included in the list (*Re Hampstead Garden Suburb Trust*, 1962). However, it may be that any alteration at all will become valid provided no objection is made in the way provided by the section, *i.e.* by an application to the court within 21 days by the holders with voting rights of 15 per cent. of the company's shares or debentures or 15 per cent. of a class of shares. On such an application, the variation will be ineffective except in so far as the court confirms it, which it may do in whole or in part and on such terms as it thinks fit.

Under section 23, if a condition in the memorandum could have been contained in the articles the above procedure may be avoided and it can be altered by special resolution unless: (i) the memorandum expressly provides for or prohibits the alteration of such a provision, or (ii) it is sought to vary or abrogate class rights, or (iii) an application is made to the court as under section 5.

# 10 Crimes and torts

As the memorandum will not specifically empower the company to engage in illegal conduct, it might be argued that all torts and crimes will be *ultra vires* and so incapable of affecting the company with legal liability. The consequence of this would be the undesirable one of allowing the company to profit from a venture whatever the methods used to make that profit. A suggested solution is to say that the *ultra vires* doctrine only invalidates *ultra vires* contractual and proprietary transactions and is inapplicable to criminal and tortious activity. This may be criticised on the ground that an action in tort could be used indirectly to enforce an invalid contract—but that is not unknown in other areas of the law, and are there perhaps reasons of public policy requiring a higher degree of responsibility for criminal or tortious conduct? A possible compromise is to say that a company should be liable for torts or crimes committed during *intra vires* activities. In practice this will generally be the case, for the traditional course of employment test will restrict potential vicarious liability in tort, and the undesirability of imposing criminal liability, unless clearly justified, will cut down the chances of its being incurred. *Mens rea* being a normal pre-requisite to liability, the scope for vicarious liability in criminal law is limited.

If criminal liability does arise it is more likely to be incurred by the company directly rather than vicariously, because the person actually committing the crime can be identified with the company as its "directing mind and will" (see page 36). Companies have thereby been held guilty of intent to deceive (*D.P.P.* v. *Kent Contractors*, 1944; *Moore* v. *Bresler*, 1944). Since the legal personality of the company is distinct from that of its members or officers, it can be guilty of conspiracy with them or others (*R.* v. *I.C.R. Haulage*, 1944—conspiracy to defraud). But it takes two to make a conspiracy and the crime cannot be committed by the company and its sole director (*R.* v. *McDonnell*, 1966). Furthermore, the Court of Appeal has recoiled from finding a conspiracy between the directors and a company which was the victim of the alleged conspiracy (*Belmont* v. *Williams*, 1978).

A company will not automatically be liable for all the criminal activities of its servants or agents. The contrary policy of the relevant legislation may be revealed as a matter of statutory interpretation. In *Tesco* v. *Nattrass* (1971), Tesco was held not liable for an assistant's display of articles for sale in contravention of the Trade Descriptions Act 1968. To hold the company liable would make illusory the statutory defence that the offence was committed due to the act or default of another person. Moreover, the Act made express provision for the liability of any director, manager, secretary or similar officer where an offence committed by a body corporate had been committed with his consent or connivance.

A servant would not usually have the necessary authority to commit a tort during an *ultra vires* activity (*Poulton* v. *L.S.W.R.*, 1867). But the company will be vicariously liable for a servant's or agent's tort committed during an *intra vires* activity if he has acted within the scope of his employment. Apart from the theories underlying the *ultra vires* doctrine, the policies of the law in tort in imposing vicarious liability may be said to justify the liability of a company which actually authorises its employee's *ultra vires* tort (*Campbell* v. *Paddington*, 1911).

# 11 Rights of members

Section 20 provides that the memorandum and articles, when registered, shall bind the company and the members as if they had been signed and sealed by each member and contained covenants by each member to observe their provisions. Thus, a member can enforce a provision enabling him to require the directors to purchase shares he wished to transfer (*Rayfield* v. *Hands*, 1959) and a company can enforce a provision requiring resort to arbitration before judicial proceedings can be taken (*Hickman* v. *Kent Sheepbreeders*, 1915).

The agreement between each of the members and the company is commonly termed a contract. Certainly it is a legally binding agreement, but one "subject to the provisions of this Act" and also to the general rules of company law. The Act does not term it a contract and, if it is one, it is a contract of a special kind. Hence, although certain contractual remedies are available (declaration; injunction; payment of a liquidated sum, *e.g.* dividends), some are not (rectification of the articles: *Scott* v. *Scott*, 1940). The courts would be reluctant to grant damages for fear of reducing capital or enabling the member to recover more than the dividends due if the regulations in the articles were observed.

It has been suggested that each member has a right to have the company's affairs conducted in accordance with the articles. This may seem somewhat contrary to the principles of majority rule (Chapter 16) but even those principles admit exceptions and the view propounded makes eminent sense in the case of small companies which are akin to partnerships.

Only the members as such can take advantage of the provisions in the articles. Thus, a director sued by the company *qua* director cannot enforce an article stipulating for arbitration, even if he is also a member (*Beattie* v. *Beattie*, 1938). And a non-member cannot enforce an article which stipulates that he should be the company solicitor (*Eley* v. *Positive Government*, 1876). There is nothing to prevent a contract being made between the company and the third party on terms incorporating the articles of association but, since the articles may by statute be varied, that contract is variable. So, for example, a contract of employment might be terminated without compensation (*Read* v. *Astoria*, 1952, p. 53). Even a contract on fixed terms cannot oust the statutory power to alter the articles but such an alteration, although effective, may constitute a breach of contract with the non-member entitling him to compensation (*Shindler* v. *Northern Raincoat*, 1960, p. 53).

*Alteration of the articles*

Section 10 provides that a company may by special resolution alter or add to its articles. The articles as varied or altered remain subject to alteration. The court may also alter the articles under section 47 of the 1980 Act, in which case the company cannot make a future inconsistent alteration without the court's leave.

The articles cannot be altered so as to produce a conflict with the memorandum unless the inconsistent provision in the memorandum could lawfully have been contained in the articles and the memorandum does not prohibit the alteration of any of its conditions. The relevant provisions in the memorandum and articles can otherwise be altered by special resolution.

Although the company is entitled to exercise fully the

rights it already has (*e.g.* to impose a lien on a member's shares: *Allen* v. *Gold Reefs*, 1900), it cannot alter the articles so as to increase the liability of a member (s. 22).

## Variation of class rights

Class rights contained in articles with no variation of rights clause may be varied if either the holders of three-quarters of the issued shares of that class consent in writing or a meeting of the class sanctions the variation by extraordinary resolution (1980 Act, s. 32(2)). If class rights are contained in the memorandum and neither the memorandum nor the articles contain a variation of rights clause, those rights may be varied if all the members agree (s. 32(5)). Often the articles include an express variation of rights clause in which case the method laid down is compulsory (s. 32(4)). In addition, section 32(2) must be satisfied where the variation is connected with the giving, variation, revocation or renewal of an authority for the allotment of securities by directors or with a reduction of capital.

Usually, if 15 per cent. of shareholders who did not consent to the variation apply to the court, a variation is ineffective unless sanctioned by the court (1948 Act, s. 72). In any event, a majority is not entitled to use its power to vary class rights in fraud on the minority; a resolution may be invalid unless passed "bona fide for the benefit of the company as a whole" (see Chap. 16). This protection may, however, be insufficient in practice. In *Greenhalgh* v. *Arderne* (1951), majority shareholders, with 50,000 votes, secured a resolution converting their 10s. shares to 2s. shares, thus ensuring their ability to prevent Greenhalgh, whose shares continued to carry 20,000 votes, from blocking any resolution they supported. They could, therefore, subsequently alter the articles to deprive Greenhalgh of a previous right of pre-emption.

A company must generally notify the Registrar of a variation of rights or the creation of a new class of shares.

# 12 Management and administration

The corporate person is separate from the servants who work work for it or the shareholders who are members of it, whether it be a small family company, the shareholders of which actively participate in decision-making and day-to-day administration, or a large industrial concern, wherein ownership (by the shareholders) and management (by the board of directors) may be largely divorced from each other. The organic structure of this corporate person and the constitutional relationship between the company's different organs are determined by the decisions of the members recorded in the articles of association and resolutions of meetings. In this fashion they determine how decisions are to be effected and how acts of the organs take effect as acts of the company itself.

The constitution is, like the company, set apart from the individual members and servants of the company. It may be changed but is fully effective until changed.

The primary organ is the *general meeting* of the shareholders. It provides the forum in which all members are prima facie entitled to participate and vote. Invariably it will devolve powers of management to another organ, the *board of directors*, but retaining the ultimate say in general policy and decision making, albeit decision making in general meeting may be manipulated by the board. Public companies must have at least two directors, the term "director" being wide enough to include anyone in accordance with whose instructions management is carried on.

The power of decision as to the following generally rests in the general meeting: winding up; changes in the memorandum and articles; payment of dividends; changes in capital structure; disposal of a substantial part of the undertaking; the appointment, remuneration, control and remuneration of directors. In addition, the general meeting can generally act where the board is unwilling or unable (*e.g.* because of deadlock) to exercise its powers (*Barron* v. *Potter*, 1914).

The relationship between the general meeting and the board is not entirely clear. In theory, the ultimate decision making power lies in the general meeting. It can override the wishes of the directors and take away from them the powers devolved to them. In practice, it tends to follow the lead suggested by the directors, so conflict is unlikely to arise. What if it does?

The older view is that the board is merely the agent of the general meeting, which can exercise the board's powers if it chooses to do so. In *Marshall's Valve Gear* v. *Manning* (1909), the board decided 2:1 not to sue a person infringing the company's patent. But the general meeting (in which the dissenting director was the majority shareholder) could sue. The modern view has developed from a case distinguished in *Marshall* on the ground that the relevant articles required an extraordinary resolution to override the board, *Automatic Self-Cleansing* v. *Cunninghame* (1906). Hence, an ordinary resolution to sell the company's undertaking was ineffective to override the board's refusal to exercise its authority to sell company property on terms it saw fit. The conclusion is that once the general meeting has devolved powers it can only exercise them itself after first taking them back from the directors.

The problem is compounded by the ambiguous but common article 80 of Table A:

> "The business of the company shall be managed
> by the directors, who may . . . exercise all such
> powers of the company as are not, by the Act
> or by these regulations, required to be exercised
> by the company in general meeting, subject,
> nevertheless, to any of these regulations, to the
> provisions of the Act and to such regulations,
> being not inconsistent with the aforesaid
> regulations or provisions, as may be prescribed
> by the company in general meeting; but no
> regulation made by the company in general
> meeting shall invalidate any prior act of the
> directors which would have been valid if that
> regulation had not been made."

If the general meeting can devolve all those powers which
it does not expressly reserve, does it follow that any
delegation under this provision must be a total delegation
unless an express reservation is made? Is it that, or merely
that the articles may expressly provide that powers cannot
be exercised by the general meeting unless first reclaimed
by alteration of the articles, that is decided by the
*Cunninghame* line of cases? Certainly, a devolution of
powers under article 80 does not permit directors to
exercise all functions of the general meeting (*e.g.* to
petition for liquidation: *Re Emmadart*, 1979).

The relationship between the two bodies is important
in connection with breaches of duty by the directors. If
they act outside their powers but *intra vires* the company,
their acts can be ratified by the company if it has full
knowledge of the circumstances (*Bamford* v. *Bamford*,
1969). But it is not clear whether the board is entitled
to postpone a decision on something prima facie within
its powers in order to obtain a prior decision on the point
by the general meeting in the exercise of a power
previously devolved to the board. It has, however, been

held that the general meeting can confer prior authority on the directors to do what is otherwise a breach of duty if the board's powers are not usurped and the notice of the meeting clearly indicates the nature of the proposed breach (*Winthrop* v. *Winns*, 1975).

*Worker participation*

Decision making is traditionally viewed from the perspectives of the owners of shares in the company (the "members" in general meeting) and the higher managerial officials (the directors). Recently attention is being focused more on the company's employees. There are a variety of ways in which company employees can more actively become involved with the prosperity which they help generate.

One method is to form a co-operative, borrowing capital at interest (possibly from the fund established under the Industrial Common Ownership Act 1976) for a venture in which they participate equally in decision making and distribution of profits. An Agency to foster their development was constituted under the Co-operative Development Agency Act 1978.

Another possibility is the establishment of a profit-sharing scheme under the Finance Act 1978, under which shares may be allocated for the sake of employees, with the benefit of certain tax concessions.

More widely known are recent proposals for the introduction of a scheme of industrial democracy, advocated by those who may wish to curb the powers of the growing managerial class, to give effect to the idea of a company as a social or economic enterprise between capitalists and workers, and/or to recognise the increased importance of plant-level collective bargaining and of consultation over confrontation.

The scheme advocated by the EEC is the establishment of a two-tier board structure, with a supervisory board of directors, nominated by shareholders and employees, which concerns itself with general policy issues and the election of a management board of directors, which is concerned with day-to-day management.

The Bullock Committee on Industrial Democracy (1977), however, recommended a unitary board structure, as an extension of collective bargaining into the company's structure. Trades unions and shareholders would each appoint X number of the directors and a balancing number, Y (which would be less than X), would be appointed jointly or, in default of agreement, by an Industrial Democracy Commission. Thus, there would be 2X + Y directors, who would have a certain number of attributed functions - so that the general meeting could not emasculate them by holding all decision making powers to itself.

*Directors*

A director need not be a member of the company. Another company may be a director. But an undischarged bankrupt cannot be a director, nor usually a person aged over 70, nor a corporation whose sole director is the company secretary. Likewise a company's secretary (which it must have) cannot be its sole director. Directors are appointed invidivually for the period specified in the articles. The court may prohibit from acting as directors: fraudulent persons, previous directors of companies which have been wound-up and are unfit to act and persons who have persistently failed to comply with requirements of the Companies Acts.

A director may have a contract of service with the company, whether as director and/or in some additional capacity. But he cannot be an auditor nor, if the sole director, the secretary. Prima facie directors must exercise their powers (unless ministerial) personally and collectively but the articles frequently authorise them to create and delegate functions to a *managing director*, who is appointed appointed directly by the board, to which he is answerable,

51

albeit (like the other directors) his duties are owed to the company. His powers may be on such terms as the board fixes from time to time or completely devolved to him until formally revoked by the board, in which case the company will have three distinct organs each with its own sphere of power.

A director ceases to hold office if: he resigns; his period of appointment under the articles or his contract terminates; or he is removed under section 184 (below). He will not necessarily vacate office because of a breach of his contract of employment, a resolution for liquidation, or the appointment of a receiver out of court whose role is not inconsistent with his. If he does lose office, he may, if so entitled, nevertheless be able to claim damages for wrongful dismissal, compensation for unfair dismissal (*Parsons* v. *Parsons*, 1979) or redundancy payment.

Section 184 empowers the company by ordinary resolution to remove a director before the expiration of his period of office, notwithstanding anything in the articles or in any agreement with him, so long as the company receives 28 days' notice of the resolutions, informs the director and circulates any representations he makes. The statutory power cannot be excluded but it may be circumvented. In *Bushell* v. *Faith* (1969), an article tripling the votes on directors' shares on a resolution to remove a director was upheld, because all the Act required was an ordinary resolution. It was silent on how many votes per share there could be. Lord Upjohn suggested that if the court were to nullify such an article (which Lord Donovan thought necessary in a family company to prevent repercussions from family quarrels in the board room) then votes should in such a case be given to share-holders who otherwise had none.

It has been suggested that a right to compensation may not be available to a managing director appointed for an unspecified term and on the basis of article 107 of Table A, which authorises the directors to appoint a managing director "on such terms as they think fit, and, subject to the terms of any agreement . . . may revoke such appointment . . . His appointment shall be automatically determined *if he cease from any cause to be a director*."

In *Nelson* v. *Nelson* (1914), it was decided that termination of a contract terminable under article 107 did not deprive the managing director from claiming damages for breach of a term for fixed duration. In *Southern Foundries* v. *Shirlaw* (1904), a managing director received damages for wrongful dismissal after the articles had been altered to enable his removal as a director, since his removal , albeit effective, was in breach of a term that he should be managing director for 10 years, which then became impossible.

*Shirlaw* was distinguished, on the basis that the contract in it was outside the articles and the power of dismissal arose after the contract was made, in *Read* v. *Astoria* (1952), wherein a managing director appointed on the basis of an article equivalent to article 107, but without a separate contract, received no damages for dismissal. But *Shirlaw* was preferred to *Read* in *Shindler* v. *Northern Raincoat* (1960).

Does, therefore, a managing director appointed on the basis of articles including one such as article 107 but without a separate contract of employment have no claim to compensation for loss of his position consequent on his ceasing to be a director? Or is article 107 merely to ensure that a person cannot be a managing director without being a director, rather than to sanction summary dismissal without compensation?

# 13 Liability for officers and agents

A contract made *by* the company itself (through one of its organs) will obviously bind it. But what of a contract made *on behalf of* the company by a person acting as an agent?

An agent who has been expressly authorised to act can bind the company with respect to matters within his *express, implied* or *usual* authority. An "agent" with no authority at all will not bind the company unless the company later *ratifies* his acts, which it will wish to do if it wants to enforce the contract. Otherwise, the party attempting to contract with the company (the "contractor") may be able to sue the agent for *breach of warranty of authority* (*Firbank's Executors* v. *Humphreys*, 1886).

An agent with no authority as described above (because he exceeds his authority or because he has been given none) or whose acts are not ratified may bind the company if he acts within his *apparent* or *ostensible* authority. He may have to indemnify the company for making it liable but the contractor can sue the company directly.

## Ostensible authority

In *Freeman* v. *Buckhurst* (1964), a company was bound by a contract entered into by a person acting as its managing director with its consent, although he had not been formally appointed. There are four conditions for such liability.

(1) A representation must be made to the contractor that the agent had authority to enter on behalf of the company into a contract of the kind sought to be enforced.

The directors are the company's usual agents and "the acts of a director or manager shall be valid notwithstanding any defect that may afterwards be discovered in this appointment" (s. 180). Even so, the directors must normally exercise their powers as a board and an individual director or other person will only be able to exercise the board's powers by delegation or by a representation to the board that the individual has authority. Such authority may usually be delegated to the managing director.

In *Panorama* v. *Fidelis* (1971), a company was bound to pay for cars hired by the company secretary, ostensibly for carrying the company's customers. The modern company secretary, being more than a mere clerk, has extensive duties and responsibilities and has authority to enter contracts for administrative purposes, without necessarily having authority relating to the commercial management of the company.

(2) The representation must be made by a person or persons having "actual" authority to manage the business of the company either generally or in respect of those matters to which the contract relates.

Thus, a director without authority cannot, by saying he has it, give himself ostensible authority. But if the board acquiesces in his exercise of such authority, the company may be bound (*Hely-Hutchinson* v. *Brayhead*, 1967). Similarly, a forged document apparently sealed or signed on behalf of the company will not bind it (*Ruben* v. *Great Fingall*, 1906) unless someone with authority represents it as the company's. A purchaser can rely on a deed executed in the presence of the secretary and a director (Law of Property Act 1925, s. 74(1)).

(3) The contractor must, by relying on the representation, be induced thereby to enter into the contract.

A contractor might argue that, since he has constructive notice of the company's public documents, he can therefore rely on a representation of authority contained therein (such as that the board may delegate certain authority to an individual director). This is wrong. He will only be able to rely on a provision therein if he has actual knowledge of it; otherwise there is no reliance (*Rama* v. *Proved Tin*, 1952).

(4) There must be no circumstance precluding the contractor's reliance.

(a) In particular, the company's public documents should not demonstrate a lack of capacity to enter the relevant contract or to delegate authority to an agent to enter it. As the contractor has constructive notice of the public documents, he is bound by limitations therein. Thus, he is deemed to know of lack of authority where it can only be given by a resolution which must be filed, and none has been. There are exceptions to this:

(i) In *Royal British Bank* v. *Turquand* (1856), the board of directors could borrow money on bond if authorised by a resolution. The lending bank could enforce such a transaction although no resolution had been passed. "Finding that the authority might be made complete by a resolution, [the contractor] would have a right to infer the fact of a resolution authorising that which on the face of the document appeared to be legitimately done." A contractor is entitled to assume that acts of "internal management" (which do not have to be made public) have been carried out.

(ii) Certain defects are expressly covered. Subject to contrary proof, minuted meetings of directors of members or directors are deemed duly held and appointments of directors and

managers deemed valid (s.145(3)). But the
contractor will not be assisted by the curing of
defects if there has been no appointment at
all (*Morris* v. *Kanssen*, 1946).

(iii) A contractor may enforce a contract "decided
on by the directors" despite restrictions on
capacity or authority of which he is unaware
(E.C.A., s.9(1)).

(b) The contractor must not have actual knowledge of
the lack of authority.

(c) The circumstances must not be such that he should
be put on inquiry. Where E.C.A., s. 9(1) applies, a contractor must act in good faith but this is presumed, unless
proved otherwise, and he is not bound to enquire into lack
of capacity or authority.

# 14 Duties of directors

Directors act as *agents*, with similar duties to, but not with all the rights of, agents. They may be employed as *servants* of the company, but as directors they have greater obligations of good faith. Their fiduciary position and their position as regards company property liken them to *trustees*, but directors' duties of care and skill are lower. The importance of their position depends not on its description but on the consequences of being directors so far as concerns the extent of their duties. Basically, a director must carry out his duties with skill and care and act bona fide in the interests of the company.

*Performance of duties generally*

A director is under a positive obligation to carry out his duties (albeit they are not generally stated with any particularity). He must not exceed his powers (although if he does, the company may still be bound) and must indemnify the company for losses incurred as a result of any breach of duty, as well as accounting to it for benefits received as a consequence of his position as director.

Although they may delegate the performance of ministerial functions to other officials, directors must not delegate the exercise of their *discretion*. This they must exercise (bona fide) as they, and not the court, think fit; nor will the court direct them to exercise discretion in a mandatory way at the instigation of shareholders (*Pergamon* v. *Maxwell*, 1970). Whatever their motives, their overriding duty to the company forbids their fettering their discretion by agreement with third parties, although an agreement between shareholder directors as to how they vote as directors may be valid. And directors who have entered into a contract on behalf of the company may be bound by a term of the contract to take steps to carry it out.

*Proper purpose*

Directors' freedom of deciding how they will exercise their powers is limited by their having to exercise them for the purposes for which they were given. Their decisions will be upheld if, as a matter of construction, they have acted within their powers (*Re Smith & Fawcett*, 1942) and if their main purpose is proper. Thus, directors who are ordinary shareholders may consider their own interests and capitalise dividends with the effect of weakening the position of preference shareholders provided that, decided objectively, their moving purpose is to benefit the company (*Mills* v. *Mills*, 1938).

Directors are commonly empowered to issue new shares, primarily in order to raise necessary new finance, albeit the need may not be critical at the time of issue. It would be improper for them to issue shares to weight the voting strength so as to defeat a take-over bid and entrench themselves in office. But such an issue was said in *Hogg* v. *Cramphorn (1967)* to be ratifiable by the general meeting and was in fact subsequently ratified. *Hogg* was not followed in *Teck* v. *Millar (1973)*, in which an issue of shares to a firm to whom certain management rights had been granted was upheld, although the existing majority shareholder, who had wished to develop the company's properties, thereby lost control. It was, said the British Columbian court, no exception to the rule requiring the directors to act in the company's interests that the majority shareholders should not be deprived of control; the directors could take account of the reputation, policies and experience of anyone seeking to take over the company.

The Privy Council in *Smith* v. *Ampol*, (1974) explained *Teck* on the basis that the directors' decision related to management (who should obtain exploitation rights?) and not control. The allotment of shares in *Ampol* to a company company which wanted to make a take-over bid, with the apparently honest intention of raising much-needed finance, was declared invalid, its effect being to reduce the majority shareholding of two other companies whose take-over bid had been rejected. Directors should not "interfere with that element of the company's constitution which is separate from and set against their powers."

Is it all open for an English court to sanction an issue of shares which has the effect of depriving majority shareholders of control even where directors are incontrovertibly acting solely for the company's best interests?

*Conflict of interest and duty*

A director should not place himself in a position in which which there does or might arise a conflict between his duties to the company and the interests of either himself or a third party. Thus, a director who has a contract of employment with his company cannot act as a director of another company, because he must not *compete* with his company. But where competition is not intended, and the presence of another company's director on the board as a non-executive director not under a contract of service might be a beneficial influence, are multiple directorships justifiable?

Equitable principles similarly discourage directors' *contracts* with their company or with third parties, even where the company benefits from them. A director who so contracts should account to the company for profits received and might even be dismissed. The company may, but need not, avoid the contract. Section 199 imposes a basic duty on a director with an interest in a present or received and might even be dismissed. The company may but need not avoid the contract. Section 199 imposes a basic duty on a director with an interest in a present or proposed contract to delcare the nature of his interest *to a board meeting*. The extent of the duty is uncertain and apparently limited but non-compliance means: a fine, the contract is voidable, and loss of the protection of an exemption clause, which might otherwise excuse him from liability. The director's means of avoiding the consequences of breach of the general rule include: disclosure, authorisation or ratification by the general meeting, or an exemption clause in the articles(although reliance on exemption clauses is subject to compliance with section 199, and general adherence to the overriding duty of good faith: section 205).

Directors' *contracts of employment* with the company are particularly prescribed, publicity being required of their terms, especially with regard to remuneration. Tax-free payments to directors are banned as is compensation for (imposed or voluntary) loss of office if not disclosed to and approved by the company (ss. 191-4). Circumvention of the latter prohibition has been condoned where payments are made in connection with loss of a different office from that of director or if the agreement to compensate antedates the loss of office (*Taupo* v. *Rowe*, 1977) but full disclosure should still be necessary.

## Loans

Loans to directors by the company are also generally not allowed except in certain cases (s. 190). Subject to the statutory restrictions, companies may make their own rules as to contracts with directors.

## Personal profits

A director, whatever his motives, should not keep personal profits which he would, or might, not have made if he had not been a director. In *Regal* v. *Gulliver* (1942) directors had to account for profits made on the sale of shares in a subsidiary, as their original opportunity to acquire the shares arose by virtue of their positions as directors, even though they acted in the company's interests and the general meeting would have ratified their actions, given the opportunity (see too *Boardman* v. *Phipps*, 1966). The cases seemed to establish that the mere fact of his having profited in such circumstances was sufficient to shew breach of duty, but recent cases suggest that he may retain profits if the company has had a complete opportunity itself to act and has, with full knowledge of the facts, renounced the opportunity and agreed to the director's personal exploitation of it (*Queensland Mines* v. *Hudson*, 1978).

*Duties of care and skill*

The director's obligation to refrain from negligence is light. Several reasons have been given: businessmen are required to take risks and are not be condemned with hindsight by a judge substituting his own, arguably uninformed, assessment of the circumstances; directors must be permitted to delegate their functions to other officials. The difficulty of proving that the director's performance would have avoided loss and the loss which would have been avoided narrows the likelihood of litigation to amplify the standard of care, the main aspects of which were laid down in *Re City Equitable Ins.* (1925): (i) A director need not exhibit in the performance of his duties a greater degree of skill than may reasonably be expected from a person of his knowledge and experience; (ii) He is not bound to give continuous attention to the affairs of his company; (iii) Subject to the articles and business practice, a reasonable delegation of duties to officials is justified.

*Beneficiaries of directors' duties*

A director does not own his duties to the board.

Otherwise, directors could sanction their fellows' breach. Duties are not owed to a particular organ of the company (albeit the general meeting may sanction what would otherwise be a breach) but to the company as a whole.

Thus in *Percival* v. *Wright* (p. 20) directors breached no duty of disclosure to shareholders who had offered them shares at an undervalue; their duty to the company required keeping secret confidential negotiations affecting the price. Owing duties to the corporate entity means that a director's duty to account for profits survives even though the shareholders at the time of breach of duty have been replaced by new ones who have arguably not suffered from the breach (*Abbey* v. *Stumborg*, 1978).

*A fortiori* a director appointed by debenture-holders generally owes no duty to them as such. The advantage to them in being able to nominate a director lies in that their nominee can help ensure that company affairs are conducted properly.

More direct duties to creditors may be held to exist, at least during winding-up (*Walker* v. *Wimborne*, 1976) and special facts may produce duties directly owed to certain shareholders. And it may be that a more modern conception of who or what a company comprises should lead directors to take more account of interests not merely of shareholders but of, *e.g.* employees.

### Effects of breach of duty

In addition to possible liability to fines or imprisonment under statute, a director may be liable to summary dismissal (s. 184).

The company may be able to rescind contracts entered into owing to his breach of duty and it may be able to claim a declaration or an injunction, to restrain breach.

The director will be personally liable to account for benefits received and will hold on a constructive trust any property belonging to the company in equity. He may also have to pay compensation or damages. For using company property for his own purposes in breach of his fiduciary duties, a director may also have to pay compound interest on sums he has to pay (*Wallersteiner v. Moir (No. 2)*, 1975). Third parties who have participated in the breach may also be liable to damages or an action for money had and received (*Mahesan v. Malaysia Housing*, 1978) or to a constructive trust (*Selangor v. Cradock (No. 3)*, 1968).

Directors may escape liability if the general meeting validly ratifies the breach or if they can claim an indemnity from the company (or if they are insured). The court has a discretion to relieve them, wholly or in part, from breach of duty if they ought in the circumstances to be excused (s. 448).

# 15 Meetings and resolutions

Fundamental decisions concerning the company's activities and future are decided, insofar as the power of decision has not been devolved on the directors, *in general meetings* of the shareholders. Usually they are confined to the single *annual general meeting (A.G.M.)* which must be held in each calendar year for declaring dividends, considering accounts and the reports of auditors and directors, and for electing directors and auditors. *Extraordinary general meetings* may be called when the need arises. Meetings of a particular class of members or creditors are called *class meetings*.

Decisions in meetings are made by resolution. An *ordinary resolution* (passed by a simple majority of votes cast by those present and entitled to vote) generally suffices. (A *written resolution* signed by all members entitled to vote may be as effective.) More important issues may have to be decided by *special resolution* (requiring 21 days' notice and a three-fourths majority of votes cast) or by an *extraordinary resolution* (requiring the same majority, plus notice).

The articles can confer or abrogate a right to call meetings. Directors are generally empowered to decide when to call them. But members holding 10 per cent. or more of the paid-up capital with voting rights who state their objects may require the directors to call an extraordinary general meeting; if the directors default, it may be convened by requisitionists representing 50 per cent. or more of the voting rights. If the A.G.M. is not held, a member may apply for it to be called by the Department of Trade. In addition to its inherent power to call meetings, the court may order one to be held and conducted in whatever manner it sees fit where it is otherwise impracticable to call one or conduct it in the prescribed manner. An auditor may requisition an extraordinary general meeting to consider the circumstances of his resignation.

The articles can determine the necessary period of notice. Each member must generally receive 14 days' notice, 21 days for the A.G.M. or of a special resolution, but general acquiescence may validate a shorter period. Notice is generally adequate if it enables a member to decide whether he ought to attend to safeguard his interests. It must indicate the time and place and, if pertinent, that it is the A.G.M. or that a special or extraordinary resolution is to be passed. *Special notice* must be given 28 days before the meeting to the company (which must notify the members: s. 142) of a resolution to remove a director or to appoint one over the retiring age, and sometimes of the appointment or removal of an auditor. An individual member cannot use this procedure merely to compel the inclusion of a resolution on the agenda (*Pedley* v. *I.W.A.*, 1977).

A sufficient proportion of members (determined by s. 140) may require the company to circulate those entitled to receive notice of the A.G.M. regarding a resolution to be moved at a meeting. But the directors have the whip hand with circulars as they generally have better opportunity to prepare them and to finance their circulation from company funds. Although participation in voting must generally be by attendance at the meeting, attendance may be by *proxies*. These are generally influenced by the directors, sending forms of appointment with the circulars representing their views. Even in the case of two-way proxies (required by the Stock Exchange for quoted companies and permitting authorisation to vote either way) members generally authorise proxies to vote with the directors.

The meeting (which should be quorate—the articles usually allow a small quorum) has as chairman a person elected by the members, generally the managing or another director.

Unless the specific form of a resolution is pre-determined in the notice of the meeting, a member may move any resolution on the subject-matter indicated in that notice. Members may speak to the motion or any permissible amendment, after which a vote is taken. A show of hands (on which proxies cannot vote), with one vote per person voting, may decide the issue. But a poll can be demanded by a specified number of shareholders (s. 137) or by the chairman, exercising his power to give effect to the true sense of the meeting. On a poll, each share generally carries one vote, but a member is not obliged to cast all his votes or to cast all those he does use the same way: hence, a nominee shareholder can give effect to the wishes of different beneficial owners.

The company must keep minutes of the meeting and these may be inspected by the members. Certain resolutions which may affect non-members must be registered and annexed to the articles, as part of the company's public documents (s. 143). They include special and extraordinary resolutions, resolutions binding particular classes of shareholders and resolutions for voluntary liquidation.

Normally, a resolution will be invalidated by non-compliance with the rules governing the conduct of meetings unless all members entitled to vote unanimously assent to the decision (*Re Duomatic*, 1969) or non-assenting members attend the meeting and acquiesce (*Re Bailey Hay*, 1971) or the result would be the same if the proper procedure were followed (*Bentley-Stevens* v. *Jones*, 1974).

# 16 Majority rule

Company decisions are taken by the members, meeting together and deciding by a majority vote. This makes sense. Decisions have to be made some way and it seems fair that the wishes of the majority should prevail (albeit the majority is generally determined by the number of shares held rather than the number of shareholders voting).

Majority rule and the existence of the company's separate legal personality produce an important consequence. In *Foss* v. *Harbottle* (1843), directors were alleged to have misapplied company property. Two share-holders wished to bring an action to make them account to the company. But they could not: the company, as the victim of the alleged misconduct, was the proper person to decide whether to sue. The continuing availability of the majority to decide the point prima facie justifies denial of interference by the minority (*Macdougall* v. *Gardiner*, 1875).

But the majority cannot go on unchecked. In *Edwards* v. *Halliwell* (1950), certain exceptions to the rule in *Foss* v. *Harbottle* were noted:

(i) It does not apply to *ultra vires* acts, which by their nature cannot be ratified by the majority.

(ii) Minority shareholders can complain of a fraud on the minority (see below).

(iii) A bare majority cannot do something needing a larger majority.

(iv) Individual members can always assert their personal
     rights.

It has been argued that every member has a right to have
the company's affairs conducted in accordance with the
regulations binding himself, the other members and the
company by virtue of section 20. Certainly he has a limited
right to a personal action if his personal rights are infringed
(*e.g.* to restrain action on the basis of a resolution regarding
which his vote is not recorded: *Pender* v. *Lushington*, 1877)
and the *Foss* rule may not apply to such an action. But it is
basically the case that his right as a member is to participate
in decisions ultimately made by the majority, so that
shareholders may be restrained from legal action, in order
to give the general meeting the opportunity to decide (*Hogg*
v. *Cramphorn*, 1966).

Provided a decision not to sue has not been made by a
majority (independant of any potential defendants) of a
competent company organ, individual shareholders may
bring a *representative* or *derivative* action in respect of a
complaint in their capacity as members of the company
(the real plaintiff) where those in control of the company
are allegedly at fault (*Atwool* v. *Merryweather* 1867). The
company itself should be made a party to the proceedings
so as to be bound by the judgment. The plaintiffs should
first seek a Master's sanction for the proceedings, to secure
their right to an indemnity from the company for costs
(*Wallersteiner* v. *Moir (No. 2)*, 1975).

Often such an action will be brought against directors
for breach of fiduciary duty. Possibly, a derivative action
for negligence cannot lie (*Pavlides* v. *Jensen*, 1956). The
contrary has been suggested in view of *Daniels* v. *Daniels*
(1978), where minority shareholders successfully pleaded
breach of duty by directors and majority shareholders who
sold  company property to a director's wife at an undervalue. But the case has been regarded merely as concerning
the obtaining of a personal advantage from the position of
the directors, as a fraud on the minority.

*Voting and fraud on the minority*

A shareholder is generally free to exercise his vote as he wishes. Thus, in *Northern Counties* v. *Jackson* (1974), a director was bound, by his duty to the company, to call a meeting and to recommend a particular resolution which the company had to pass, or be in contempt of court: but as a shareholder he was entitled to vote against it. If he wishes, a shareholder may contract to exercise his vote in a particular way.

The fact that the company is merely the object of the free collective will exercised by the members does not mean that there are no restraints *inter se* on their voting. Minority shareholders can restrain the majority from depriving the company of property it owns or advantages owed to it, such as the opportunity of particular contracts. Secondly, the general meeting cannot generally relieve directors of liability for impending or past breaches of duty except where it is apprised of the full facts and acts bona fide in the interests of the company (*Hogg* v. *Cramphorn*, 1966; *Bamford* v. *Bamford*, 1969). Thus, it cannot authorise or ratify "fraudulent" conduct (*Atwool* v. *Merryweather*, 1867).

Thirdly, the majority can be restrained from altering the articles of association to buy out the minority where they are merely acting to further their own capricious interests (*Dafen* v. *Llanelly*, 1907; *Brown* v. *British Abrasive Wheel*, 1919). But the court is not entitled to prevent the majority's action if it cannot otherwise be shewn not to be bona fide in the company's interests (*Shuttleworth* v. *Cox*, 1927). When is a variation of class rights permissible? If it is in the interests of an individual hypothetical member (in which case do shareholders owe any duties to the other members?)? Or so long as there is no discrimination against minorities (arguably the result of any majority decision)? Does the "contract of membership" under section 20 confer duties as well as rights?

In *Clemens* v. *Clemens* (1976), a 55 per cent. shareholder voted for an alteration of the memorandum which would permit the introduction of a share incentive scheme for employees and would simultaneously reduce her niece's 45 per cent. shareholding to 25 per cent. The judge set the resolution aside on the basis that the majority shareholder's aim was to prevent her niece's ever gaining control (by exercising her right of pre-emption) and that shareholders' rights are subject to equitable considerations which may make it unjust to exercise them in a particular way. If this is true, to what extent can such a consideration be applied to companies with a larger more diverse membership?

# 17 Publicity

English company law persistently requires disclosure of certain details, whether to the public or to particular individuals or groups of individuals, so that persons have sufficient information to enable them to decide whether to act or to refrain from acting in a particular way.

Information may be made available in different ways to different individuals. A company could publicise as many details about its affairs as it wished but, like most natural persons, it will prefer to keep them private. If it wishes its shares to be listed on the Stock Exchange, it will have to undertake to provide the Exchange with information which can be made generally available.

Lower minimal standards are currently laid down by the law, which requires specified matters to be registered and made open to public inspection, *e.g.* the memorandum, the articles, special resolutions, names of officers and details of share capital. In addition, the Registrar must gazette notice of certain documents he issues or registers (E.C.A., s. 9(3)). Other information must be maintained by the company, *e.g.* the minutes of meetings. Some of this information may be inspected by the public (normally, the information that is also available at the Companies Registry), some by the members (*e.g.* minutes of general meetings) and some only by the directors (*e.g.* books of account). But a right of inspection may be restricted. The court may refuse to allow a director to inspect the account books, a right which he holds for the benefit of the company, where it would be injurious to the company (*Conway* v. *Petronius*, 1978).

Bare information may be of little use except to those with professional advisers able to assess and explain its significance. In such cases, another source of publicity, the financial press, may play a useful role in exposing facets of a company's dealings.

This may well be so with company *accounts*. The directors must (1976 Act, s. 1), in respect of each accounting reference period, prepare a *profit and loss account* and a *balance sheet* (both of which must give a true and fair view of the company's affairs at the end of its financial year. These must be accompanied by a *directors' report* (with respect to the state of the company's affairs and the recommended dividend) and the auditors' report. Holding companies must have group accounts. The accounts must be sent to the members, then laid before the general meeting; copies must be delivered to the Registrar. Accounting records must also be kept at the company's offices (1976 Act, s. 12).

The accuracy of the accounts must be verified by independent *auditors* (accountants) appointed by the general meeting. They must examine the accounts and are empowered to obtain necessary information for that purpose. They must decide whether proper accounting records have been kept and whether those agree with the profit and loss account and balance sheet, and must report to the members, stating whether the accounts have been properly prepared and whether they give a true and fair view of the matters concerned (1967 Act, s. 14). An auditor may be removed by ordinary resolution, in which case he may be heard on the matter at any relevant general meeting (1976 Act, s. 14). If he resigns, he must state whether or not this is because of circumstances of which the members should know (s. 16). If it is, he may requisition an extraordinary general meeting to receive and consider his explanations (s. 17).

*Inspections and investigations*

The Department of Trade may require the production of company books or accounts (1967 Act, s. 109). It can also appoint an inspector to investigate and report on a company's affairs where it appears there are circumstances suggesting that its business has been or is being conducted fraudulently or oppressively, or that officers have been guilty of misconduct or members have not been given information they are entitled to expect (1948 Act, s. 165(*b*)). The company and the members may be able to require or request an investigation but they normally invite the Department to decide. The Department is also empowered to investigate the company's ownership.

The threat of an investigation may deter undesirable conduct, but the appointment of an inspector supposedly carries no adverse implication, so he is not bound by the rules of natural justice (*Norwest* v. *D.T.I.*, 1978), although he must act fairly (*Re Pergamon*, 1970). The inspector may inform the Department of suspected offences and he must report to the Department, which may bring civil proceedings on behalf of the company or petition under section 47 of the 1980 Act or for a winding-up (1967 Act, s. 35).

These legal powers underpin the voluntary system of regulation provided by the Stock Exchange and the Council for the Securities Industry.

# 18 Liquidations

A company may be wound-up by three methods (s. 211).
1. *Compulsory liquidation*

The court may be petitioned by: the company; any
creditor who establishes a prima facie case; *contributories*
(those shareholders who must contribute to the company's
assets on liquidation: ss. 212-213); the Department of
Trade; or the Official Receiver. The grounds are that: the
company has so resolved; it has not commenced business
within a year of incorporation or has not carried on
business for a year; the number of members has fallen
below the statutory minimum; it is unable to pay its debts;
or it is just and equitable to wind it up (s. 222).

The "just and equitable" ground enables the court to
subject the exercise of legal rights to equitable considerations. It can take account of personal relationships of
mutual trust and confidence in small companies, particularly where an understanding that all members may
participate in the business is breached (*Ebrahimi* v.
*Westbourne Galleries*, 1972). Thus, an order may be made
where the majority deprive the minority of their right to
appoint and remove their own director (*Re A & BC*, 1975).

Once liquidation begins, generally when the petition is
presented, dispositions of company property become void
and litigation involving the company is generally restrained.

The court may dismiss the petition or make a winding-up
order. It is empowered to appoint an official receiver and
one or more liquidators and has general powers to enable

rights and liabilities of claimants and contributories to be settled. Separate meetings of creditors and contributories must decide whether to apply for the appointment of a liquidator and possibly of a *committee of inspection* (of their representatives) to act with him.

## 2. *Voluntary liquidation*

Voluntary liquidation begins when the company so resolves, whence it generally ceases to carry on business. If the directors have previously made a declaration of the company's solvency, it is a members' voluntary winding-up. If not, it is a creditors'; if so, a meeting of creditors must be called, to which the directors must report on the company's affairs. A liquidator must, and a committee of inspection may, be appointed. A compulsory liquidation order is still possible, but a petitioning contributory would need to satisfy the court that a voluntary liquidation would prejudice the contributories.

## 3. *Winding-up subject to the supervision of the court*

This is of minimal importance.

### Liquidators

In a compulsory liquidation, the liquidator must assume control of all property to which the company appears entitled. He must have regard to directions of contributories and creditors, keep proper records, and deliver accounts to the Department of Trade, which has supervisory powers over him.

In a voluntary liquidation, a liquidator who doubts the company's solvency must call a meeting of creditors. At its conclusion, he must present accounts to a general meeting and, if a creditors' voluntary liquidation, to a meeting of creditors.

In addition to his statutory duties, the liquidator owes fiduciary duties to the company, whose agent he is. In a compulsory liquidation, he may be empowered to engage in litigation in the company's name, carry on such of the company's business as is necessary and pay or enter any compromise or arrangement with creditors and can do all things to wind-up the company's affairs and distribute its assets.

## Priority of claims

Before claims are met, creditors are entitled to enforce their secured claims against company property subject to fixed charges to the extent their claims may so be met: thereafter, they rank as unsecured creditors. The costs of liquidation must be met first out of the company's remaining assets. Next rank (*pari passu*) certain preferential payments: rates falling due within the previous 12 months; all taxes then due (not exceeding one year's assessment); wages due to junior employees in the preceding four months (up to £800 per employee) and accrued holiday remuneration for employees (payments for these may be claimed by the D.H.S.S. and third parties who have already paid the money); and (except in voluntary liquidations for the purposes of reconstruction) employers' and employees' contributions under social security legislation. Claims of debenture-holders with floating charges are postponed to the preferential creditors. Debts provable in bankruptcy are then paid *pari passu*. All remaining debts are then paid. Finally, the company's assets are divided amongst the members according to their rights (in the articles) on liquidation. No provision is necessary for untraced shareholders (*Re Electricidad*, 1978). Unclaimed assets are paid into the Bank of England's Insolvency Services Account.

## Dissolution

Having wound up the company's affairs, the liquidator may apply to the court for an order for dissolution. But an application may be made to the court within the following two years for the dissolution to be declared void, although acts done in the meanwhile will not thereby be validated.

### Striking off the register

Cheaper than liquidation and formal dissolution is an application to the Registrar for the company to be struck off the register. He may do this if he has reasonable cause to believe that the company is not carrying on business or has been wound up and, after enquiry, no cause is shewn why it should not be struck off. This procedure will not avail those wishing to deprive members and creditors of the protection afforded to them in liquidation.

### Misconduct

Any act done relating to company property within six months of liquidation may be deemed a *fraudulent preference* and be invalid accordingly (s. 320), although an act is not a fraudulent preference merely because one creditor happens to have been preferred to another.

If, during liquidation, it appears that any business of the company has been carried on for any fraudulent purpose, the court may declare those involved to be liable without limit for all or any of the company's debts or liabilities (s. 332). Actual fraud must be proved but it is sufficient for the *fraudulent trading* to have occurred on one occasion only (*Re Gerald Cooper*, 1978).

The 1948 Act imposes criminal liability for certain offences committed in connection with liquidations.

### Unfair prejudice

The 1980 Act, s. 47 provides a possible alternative remedy to winding-up. Any member complaining that, by way of any act or omission, the company's affairs are being or would be conducted in a manner unfairly prejudicial to himself and (possibly) other members may petition the court. So may the Department of Trade. If the petition appears well founded the court may give such relief as it thinks fit. It may regulate the company's future affairs; require it to take or refrain from taking particular action; or provide for the purchase of a member's shares. If the court's order operates to alter the company's memorandum or articles, no future inconsistent alteration may be made without its leave.

A member may not obtain relief if he is not being oppressed *qua* member. Mere prejudice, without its being unfair, would be insufficient: *e.g.* the mere use by the majority of its majority power. So, the drawing by a director who is a majority shareholder of remuneration to which he is not entitled is not enough, unless he uses his voting strength to procure or retain it (*Re Jermyn Street Baths*, 1971).

# 19 Arrangements and reconstructions

## Introduction

By the Industry Act 1975, a National Enterprise Board was set up with power to promote and support schemes for take-overs and mergers, to help rationalise and reorganise British industry. But the Act also empowers the Secretary of State to prevent control of manufacturing undertakings passing to foreign residents and to acquire the capital or assets of such undertakings where such control has passed or may pass.

Under the Fair Trading Act 1973, the Director-General of Fair Trading may refer to the Monopolies and Merger Commission for investigation and report where it appears that two or more companies (one of which is U.K. based) have ceased or may cease to be distinct enterprises, so that 25 per cent. or more of certain goods and services will be supplied by or to one person or that the value of the assets taken over or to be taken over exceeds £5 million. The Commission reports whether this is true, whether it is against the public interest and what action should be taken. The Secretary of State may then prevent or undo the merger.

The City Code on Take-Overs and Mergers (revised 1976) imposes certain standards on take-over bids to ensure adequate disclosure and fair dealings.

## 1. *Variation of class rights*

This may be a necessary preliminary to one of the following schemes.

## 2. *Reduction of capital: sections 66-71*

If authorised by the articles, a company may by special resolution reduce its share capital. The resolution is ineffective until confirmed by the court and a copy of the court's order and a minute of the company's new share structure is registered with the Registrar. Any creditor is prima facie entitled to object, so the court should first ensure that all creditors have consented or that their claims have been met or secured. The courts generally only require compliance with the minimum legal requirements.

Hence, in *Scottish Insurance* v. *Wilsons & Clyde* (1949), the company's colliery was nationalised and it was proposed to go into liquidation. The preference shareholders were first validly paid off according to their class rights, with the result that all the compensation for nationalisation accrued to the benefit of the ordinary shareholders.

But a reduction which is patently unfair may not be confirmed. In *Re Holder's Trust* (1971), a proposal to cancel cumulative preference shares in exchange for unsecured loan stock was rejected by the court because the majority preference shareholders who secured the passing of the extraordinary resolution of the class were acting in their interests as majority ordinary shareholders rather than as members of the class and the minority had shewn the reduction to be unfair.

## 3. *Compromises, arrangements and reconstructions*

Sections 206-208 provide some control of compromises of disputed claims of the company's creditors and of arrangements modifying the rights of creditors or members, *e.g.* by dividing shares into different classes or by consolidating shares of different classes. A scheme may be proposed between the company and all of its creditors or members, or a class of either of them.

A member or creditor who is directly affected (or the liquidator) may apply to the court, which can order a meeting of the class affected. The notice of such a meeting must explain the effect of the scheme and, especially, its effect on the interests of any directors or trustees for debenture-holders concerned.

The scheme will be effective if: (i) it is voted for by three-fourths in value of those present at the meeting and entitled to vote; (ii) the court sanctions the scheme; and (iii) the Registrar receives a copy of the court's order.

The court must first ensure that the correct procedure has been followed. It will then generally assume that the scheme is fair, having been passed by the majority. It may decline to sanction it if the objective reasonably intelligent member of the class, acting from his own interests, might not approve.

In *Re Hellenic* (1975), it was proposed to cancel the ordinary shares of Hellenic and to issue new ones to Hambros, thus making it a wholly owned subsidiary of Hambros. The price offered for the shares by Hambros was fair but N.B.G. (which owned 14 per cent. of them) would become liable to pay heavy capital gains tax in Greece. The scheme received the necessary majority but was not sanctioned by the court because the class meeting voting for it was held to be improperly constituted, as it included a shareholder (with 41 per cent. of the shares) which was already a wholly owned subsidiary of Hambros and so, it was said, a separate class!

The judge also said N.B.G. could have defeated a compulsory purchase of its shares under section 209 (below) because it had more than 10 per cent. of the shares—but is that relevant to sections 206-208? Even under section 287 (below) a dissentient shareholder can only insist on being bought out, not on blocking a scheme.

Where the whole or part of a company's undertaking or property is to be transferred to another company, the court has additional powers to facilitate the transfer: *e.g.* to allot securities in the original company to the other one.

## 4. *Acquisition of dissenters' shares: section 209*

Where, under a scheme or contract, shares or a class of shares are transferred to a single "transferee" company and the holders of 90 per cent. in value of the shares to be transferred approve within four months, the transferee company then has two months in which is can notify the dissenting shareholder that it desires to acquire his shares.

If so, it becomes prima facie entitled and bound to acquire those shares on the same terms on which the shares of the other shareholders are to be transferred. In *Re Carlton* (1971), underwriters, on behalf of the transferee company, made an original offer to shareholders in the transferor company of either shares in the transferee company or a cash sum (from the underwriters). When the transferee company later came to exercise its rights under section 209, it had to offer the same terms to the minority, so that they could opt for the cash alternative.

Dissenting minority shareholders have a right within one month of notification of the transferee company's intention to acquire their shares to apply to the court, which may disallow the acquisition. Thus, objection may be made where the 90 per cent. holding was acquired by the transferee company as a result of the accepting shareholders being misled (*Gething* v. *Kilner*, 1971).

In *Re Bugle* (1961), the majority shareholders in one company formed a second company to which they transferred their shares so that the second company could acquire the shares of the minority in the original company. The court would not let section 209 be used for the purpose of getting rid of an unwanted minority.

A transferee company acquiring a 90 per cent. shareholding must notify the minority of this, so that the latter can insist on its acquiring their shares on similar terms or as the court thinks fit.

### 5. *Arrangements by liquidators: section 287*

In a members' voluntary liquidation, where it is proposed to sell or transfer the whole or part of a company's undertaking or property to another ("transferee") company, the liquidator may, if authorised by special resolution, receive as part or whole of the consideration shares or other interests in the transferee company, or he may enter into an arrangement whereby the members may, in addition to or in lieu of receiving such interests, receive other benefits from the transferee company.

The liquidator is otherwise bound by the rules governing members' voluntary liquidations and must accord creditors and members their normal rights: *e.g.* members' rights to participate in the consideration received depend on their rights in such liquidations. Any member who dissents from the proposal may, within seven days, require the liquidator in writing not to proceed or to purchase his interest before proceeding.

The court is not required to sanction the scheme and will only be involved if a member applies to it to have his rights upheld or if an application is made for compulsory liquidation; the latter may be done within a year of the special resolution, which will then be void unless sanctioned by the court. Otherwise, any sale or arrangement under section 287 binds all members and creditors.

If a scheme which comes within the terms of section 287 cannot be carried out (*e.g.* because the necessary special resolution fails), the court may sanction it under section 206 although, if it does, it can require that dissentients receive the protection they would do under section 287 (*Re Anglo-Continental*, 1922). However, it was held in *Re General Motor Cab* (1913) that if the scheme is really a sale, then section 287 must be used, not section 206.

### 6. *Other compromises and arrangements in liquidation*

With the sanction of:

(i) an extraordinary resolution of the company in a
        members' voluntary liquidation (s. 303), or
(ii) the court, the committee of inspection or a
        meeting of creditors in a creditors' voluntary
        liquidation (s. 303), or
(iii) the court or the committee of inspection in a
        compulsory liquidation (s. 245),
the liquidator may enter into any compromise or arrangement with creditors.

Any arrangement entered into between a company
about to be, or in the course of being, wound up binds the
company if sanctioned by an extraordinary resolution, and
the creditors if acceded to by three-forths in number and
value, subject to the court's power to amend, vary or
confirm on appeal by any creditor or contributory
(s. 306).

The liquidator cannot exercise his power under section
245 to distribute assets other than according to the
creditors' rights; section 206 must be used, under which
dissenting creditors have a right to object (*Re Trix*, 1970).

# Index